Understanding and
Enjoying the Bible

© Day One Publications 2005
First printed 2005

ISBN 1 903087 80-5

9 781903 087800

Unless otherwise stated, all Scripture quotations are from the
New International Version copyright © 1986

British Library Cataloguing in Publication Data available

Published by Day One Publications
Ryelands Road, Leominster, HR6 8NZ
☎ 01568 613 740 FAX 01568 611 473
email—sales@dayone.co.uk
web site—www.dayone.co.uk
North American—e-mail—sales@dayonebookstore.com
North American—web site—www.dayonebookstore.com

Designed by Steve Devane and printed by Gutenberg Press, Malta

Contents

Acknowledgements

I am deeply grateful to Andrew Anderson, Phil Arthur, Robin Dowling and Brian Edwards for their comments on the manuscript of this book. All are busy men and I have greatly appreciated their help and encouragement. Of course, I alone am responsible for the final text. I would like to thank Bishop Timothy Dudley-Smith for permission to quote from his acrostic version of Psalm 25. I am also grateful for the prodding of the Theological Team of the Fellowship of Independent Evangelical Churches, now the Affinity Theological Team, who have had 'Hermeneutics' on their agenda for a long time. What was originally envisaged has been considerably altered, but I hope this slim volume will, under God, meet a real need, especially among lay preachers and church members, but perhaps also as early reading for students and a refresher for pastors. My wife, Mary, is a constant support and encouragement and bears the burden of reading what I write in its earliest rough-hewn state.

This book is about understanding the Bible. Its purpose is to help those who read the Bible come to a clearer view of its meaning. It is intended for all those who read it regularly and would like some guidance in getting the most out of the Word of God. It covers some of the basic principles and practices of interpreting the Bible. While attempting to be straightforward it is hoped that it will enable those who struggle with some of the more difficult parts of the Bible to see how to approach them and to gain some help from them.

There are sixty-six books in the Bible, written over a period of some 1500 years. The Old Testament was written in Hebrew (there is a small amount of Aramaic in Ezra and Daniel), and the New Testament in Greek. Some of the books differ widely in their literary form, so they require different strategies of reading if they are to be understood as clearly as possible. A letter is not poetry, and poetry is not narrative, and narrative is not legislation. God has given us a wonderful variety in the Bible—a variety that enlarges our understanding and enhances our enjoyment, but that also means that we must be sensitive to the form of the book or passage.

The way *Understanding and enjoying the Bible* tackles interpretation is by looking first of all at one of the most well-known passages in the Bible, Psalm 23. The plan is to embark together on a practical exercise of trying to see how we can get the most out of that psalm. Of course, as we are looking just at one psalm, which is written as Hebrew poetry, we shall need to comment on other passages and other literary forms as we go along. This means that as the book progresses we shall need to go on to draw more general principles and look at other biblical passages. However, focussing on a particular passage provides a valuable way into the art of reading the Bible.

Sometimes people ask whether there is a particular way in which we have to read the Bible. 'The Bible,' they say, 'is God's Word, so shouldn't we read it in a different way from any other book?' There isn't a simple answer to this. If the question means that we should try to find some hidden meaning that is only there because this is the Bible, we would have to answer, 'No.' God used people who wrote in the conventions of ordinary literature to give us his Word. He accommodated himself to us by giving us a book that speaks in a way we understand. But it is also true that because God speaks to us in the Bible those who want to know what he has to say will read with a special interest and greater desire to understand. A love letter is not read in the same way as a circular from the local council. Christians love their Father and take a special delight in what he says, 'Oh, how I love your law! I meditate on it all day long' (Psalm 119:97).

There is a second way in which Christians will read the Bible in a different way from other books. 'All Scripture is God-breathed and is useful for teaching, rebuking, correcting and training in righteousness, so that the man of God may be thoroughly equipped for every good work' (2 Timothy 3:16–17). Christians know that the Bible is directed to us all, and that it has a bearing on our understanding and our living. It is not simply leisure time reading, though it can be used in that way. It does not just contain good stories which we can escape into for a while, though there are good stories in it. Nor is it merely an intellectual exercise, though it is mind-stretching in places. The Bible instructs our minds in the ways of God, it warms our hearts, it guides our lives, it is immensely devotional and practical.

Not long ago I listened to a pastor from Spain speaking about the work of the gospel in that land. He was talking particularly about those who come from other countries to work there. He emphasized the importance, not simply of acquiring a working knowledge of the Spanish language, but of getting into the Spanish mind-set. In order to understand how Spanish people 'tick' and to be able to communicate effectively with them, he said, you need to enter their world of understanding. I felt I had some understanding of what he was talking about as my parents worked for many years in Spain, and I think it would be true to say that they had gone a long way in that direction. This was especially true of my mother who had a special rapport with Spaniards and who seemed to find it easier to express herself in Spanish than English.

We need to approach the Bible in a similar way. Most of us necessarily read our Bibles in English. Nevertheless we soon realise that we are reading a book that belongs to another time and another place. It was written by people, and originally for people, who belonged to a world different in many ways from our own world. In order to understand the Bible fully we need, as far as we can, to get into that world, to understand the mind-set of the people of Bible times.

I have used the idea of three worlds rather than just one in this book.

There is nothing original about this, it is simply a way in considering how to understand the Bible which I think is helpful. So the book is divided into three sections: The world behind the text, the world within the text, and the world in front of the text.

The first thing to do is to say something about the word 'text'. By text is simply meant a piece of writing. It can be long—a whole book, or short—a particular verse in the Bible. It can refer to the whole Bible. The emphasis is on the written form, the actual writing itself—the text. Whatever may be said about background, or author, or the first readers, the one thing that is of fundamental importance is the written text, the Scripture. The word 'scripture' simply means 'writing'.

By 'world behind the text' is meant the whole background in which the particular writing was produced. This is the world of the author: the culture in which he lived, the customs of his day, the problems that confronted him. History, geography, sociology, theology and other disciplines all throw their own light on the text.

'The world within the text' refers to what the text actually says. We may know virtually nothing about the author or the background of the text, we may have no expectation of what the text says or means, but it is there to speak for itself. To look at the world within the text involves considering its literary form. It includes examining paragraphs and sentences, words and their meaning, and the way in which these are put together (or 'syntax').

'The world in front of the text' refers to the impact and effect of the text on its readers. Looking at this means considering how the text functioned when it was first received and read, how over the centuries God's people have understood it, and what it means for today. The whole question of applying the Word of God written at least 2,000 years ago to the world of today comes under this heading.

Another way of expressing this is to speak of looking at the Bible from three different perspectives. We look at the Bible—or, rather, one of its passages—in its setting; then we focus in and look directly at what it actually says, and finally we stand back and see what it all means for us and our lives. Of course, there is an inevitable overlap between these three ways of looking at the Bible. They are not watertight compartments, but they are sufficiently distinct for our purpose.

Introduction

Sometimes it is said that the way to get to the meaning of the Bible is to proceed from what it meant at the time it was written to what it means now; from the past to the present. There is value in that comment, but it does depend on one's purpose in reading. The purpose of *Understanding and enjoying the Bible* is to help those who read the Bible to come to a fuller, an all-round, deeper understanding. So, in general terms, looking at the past is very important. But it may not be important on a particular occasion. If I am lying in bed feeling unwell and turn to a psalm to help me draw near to God and receive some word from him, I don't need to trouble myself about the 'world behind the text' (though if I'm already aware of that world it will probably be an unconscious help to me). If I have to give a talk on the subject 'You shall not steal', there is also probably no need for me to spend time on the 'world behind the text', or 'the world within the text'. It is the contemporary application of the words which is clearly the important thing. But if you want the fullest understanding of the Bible, wherever you start, you will need to give attention to all three of these 'worlds'.

Part I

The world behind the text

Not long ago my wife and I walked by the side of Tarn Hows in the Lake District. There, in the half-hearted sunshine, were several sheep lying on the lush grass beside the unruffled water of the tarn. Sheep safely grazing: a perfect illustration of verse two of Psalm 23, *He makes me lie down in green pastures, he leads me beside quiet waters*. Or so it seemed. Yet it would be misleading to use this picture in trying to understand the psalm. These sheep were fenced in. They were in no danger at all, unless some tourist let his dog off the lead! But worse than that from the point of view of the psalm—there was no shepherd. The sheep needed no one to be with them, to watch over them and care for them. Even if they had been grazing freely on the fells, the picture would still have differed from that of the eastern shepherd with his sheep. So we will need to look at the psalm more closely.

Chapter 1

The shepherd and his sheep

The LORD is my shepherd, I shall not be in want.

When you read this Psalm it is almost certainly the picture of a shepherd with his sheep that automatically comes to mind. It is likely also that you will see immediately that the main thought is the care that the shepherd has for the sheep, a care so complete that *I shall not be in want*. But it is important to know that in at least three significant respects the picture differs from that of the modern, western shepherd and his sheep. The first difference is that David's picture is of sheep that were vulnerable and exposed to danger. As the psalm indicates there were dangers from steep valleys, and perhaps, at times, from rushing streams. More than that, there were wild animals always glad of an easy meal; a lion, a bear or a wolf (1 Samuel 17:34–35; John 10:12). There were human predators as well: thieves, bandits, marauding enemies from the countries around Israel looking for flocks or crops they could steal (John 10:8,10; Judges 6:4,11). All very different from woolly flocks in green fields with fences round them, though not quite so different from sheep in more mountainous areas.

The second difference is that the shepherd was out on the hills with the sheep, watching over them day and night. The very first time we ever hear about David we read, '"There is still the youngest," Jesse answered, "but he is tending the sheep." Samuel said, "Send for him"' (1 Samuel 16:11). The shepherd was out where the sheep were (cf. Luke 2:8), to protect them and to guide them: *I will fear no evil, for you are with me* (v. 4). The third difference is that the shepherd was leading the sheep, rather than driving them as shepherds do today: *he leads me* (v. 2). This meant that the sheep were safe when they followed the shepherd. They learnt to recognize his voice, to respond to his call and follow where he led (John 10:27). These points are well-known, but the lesson is important: do not jump to conclusions from your own experience about what the Bible is saying. You need to discover what the biblical picture really is. In this case other parts of

Scripture which speak of sheep and shepherds are very useful. Comparing Scripture with Scripture is a basic principle of interpretation. Books which explain the background, such as Bible dictionaries or commentaries, are also very helpful. The primary task, though, is to think carefully about the particular passage you are reading. What is it actually saying? Does it fit in with what I expect? Are there things I need to discover about the background which will give me a clearer understanding of what is being said?

A selective picture

If you think about it, this picture of the shepherd is actually a selective one. The process of selectivity is one that is likely to go on in your mind without you realizing it. Automatically you reduce the role of the shepherd to the care of the sheep—for this is what the psalm is clearly about. But it would be possible to ask why the shepherd has a flock of sheep in the first place. Does he own them because he wants their wool; because he milks them and makes cheese for his family and to be sold? Are the sheep due to be slaughtered, either for food or sacrifice? By focusing on the wool and milk it would be possible to change the picture into one in which the sheep are to serve the shepherd. Instead of the emphasis being on the shepherd providing for the sheep, it would be on the sheep providing for the needs of the shepherd. The application would then be on the importance of our service for the Lord, producing in our lives those acts and attitudes that he is looking for. It would be possible to go even further and suggest that the sheep might have been destined for sacrifice at the tabernacle and so we should render sacrificial service. But such interpretations of Psalm 23 would be without foundation. There is nothing in the psalm itself to suggest them, all the stress is on what the shepherd does for the sheep. So be careful in the interpretation and application of Scripture. It is all too possible to extend an illustration, or press a passage, beyond what Scripture is actually saying.

The ideal shepherd

David, of course, says, *The LORD is my shepherd*. We tend to start off with the shepherd/sheep idea, but the interpreter must be sensitive to what the author is saying. David puts the emphasis on the LORD. He is the one who shepherds him. David doesn't recognize any human being as his shepherd, not Saul as king, nor even Samuel, God's prophet. He has no time for, or trust in, the gods worshipped by other nations. The thought probably is, then, that the LORD is the ideal shepherd. Over against all other possible shepherds, here is the best shepherd of all. Supreme care and provision is found with the LORD: *I shall not be in want.*

Beyond the picture of the shepherd and his sheep

So it is important not to jump to conclusions from our own knowledge of shepherding in the western world in the present day. Of course, with many of us this may not be real knowledge at all, simply ideas we have picked up which may be more or less accurate. This principle applies to the whole of the Bible. Be cautious about other occupations and customs which you find in the Bible. Take, as another example, slavery in New Testament days. Such slavery was very different from the slave trade of the eighteenth century, when Africans were transported in appalling conditions to the American colonies. Consider this quotation:

Both terms (the Greek words *oiketes* and *doulos*) have also been translated 'slave' (NIV), but the horrible degradation of slaves in 19th-century America gives the word 'slave' a far worse connotation than is accurate for most of the society to which Peter was writing. Although mistreatment of slaves could occur then too, it must be remembered that 1st-century slaves were generally well treated and were not only unskilled labourers but often managers, overseers, and trained members of the various professions (doctors, nurses, teachers, musicians, skilled artisans). There was extensive Roman legislation regulating the treatment of slaves. They were normally paid for their services and could expect eventually to purchase their freedom'.[1]

Grudem probably overstates his case because there could be extreme cruelty shown to slaves in New Testament times. Nevertheless what he has to say about the type of profession a slave might have and the payment of slaves is important for our understanding. Slavery in Old Testament times was different again, though here we are given much more information in the Bible itself; and slavery in Israel differed from what happened in other nations. In other words take care to find out the background of different parts of the Bible, insofar as this is possible.

Selectivity again

We noticed that the picture of the shepherd is actually a selective one, the focus is on only one aspect of shepherding. This is a point to remember in other places. For instance, when Paul says in Philippians 3:2, 'Watch out for those dogs', what does he have in mind? Quite clearly he is not referring to animals, but rather those he calls *evil workers* who were advocating circumcision for Gentile Christians. But why *dogs*? We are likely to think of dogs biting; some houses still have notices on the garden gate, 'Beware of the dog'. But it is unlikely that Paul was thinking in those terms. Nor is he being plain rude! At that time Jews applied the word *dogs* to Gentiles, and even to lapsed Jews, because they were considered ritually unclean. Here Paul is turning the word back on these Judaizers, as they are called. They are the ones who are unclean and so outside the boundary of God's people. The picture is a selective one: not every canine quality is in view.

The same thing is clear in the parable of Jesus usually known as the parable of the unjust steward (Luke 16:1–13). The point is not that the steward was unjust, but that he acted shrewdly, and that, very often, the children of light do not act shrewdly. They can learn from him that they should act carefully and wisely, especially with their worldly wealth, making friends for eternity.

Idealization

In speaking as he does about the LORD, David shows him to be the ideal shepherd. This is an important point which is helpful in a number of respects. Some have found it difficult to see how David can really point forward to Jesus Christ as king in view of his adultery with Bathsheba, and his responsibility for the death of Uriah. The same problem arises with Solomon, with his many wives and concubines and his lapse into idolatry at the end of his life. But Jesus as Christ, the anointed one, is the true King, the ideal king, he is all that a king should be. David is a picture of Christ as a victorious king, but he was not the perfect king himself. His very sins show the need for the perfect king to come. Solomon is a king of peace with widespread prosperity throughout his kingdom, but he is not perfect either. There is only one who fulfils the ideal of kingship perfectly and that is Jesus Christ. The same is true if we think of the priests; they all failed, they needed to offer for their own sins. They pointed to the need for a perfect priest. So it was with the prophets. It is true that their words were given under the inspiration of the Holy Spirit, and so they were always accurate and reliable. But there was always a discrepancy between their words and what they were. Only one could be the Prophet, the one who not only spoke the word but was the Word, the very embodiment of truth.

Comparison and contrast

Another way of looking at this is to think of the contrasts as well as the comparisons. There are points of comparison between the eastern shepherd and the LORD as shepherd, and that is what we naturally think about. But in fact there are always contrasts. The earthly shepherd is never the same as the heavenly, nor the earthly father as the heavenly Father, nor is the earthly Jerusalem really a holy city, while the heavenly Jerusalem certainly is (Revelation 21:2,10).

We have to do the same kind of thing when we think of God as Father. It is true that comparing human fatherhood can help in understanding God the Father in relation to the Son, and in his relationship to believers as his adopted children. But those who teach children always have to be aware that there are fathers who are not good models of fatherhood at all, so that in some cases speaking of God as Father can be a hindrance rather than a help. The fact is that fatherhood is only truly seen in God, human fatherhood since the Fall is always a pale imitation of the real thing. Do not think that God is made in our image; men and women have been made in his image, not the other way round. So a shepherd's care for his sheep is an inadequate and partial illustration of the immense and glorious care that God has for those who trust him

Note

1   **Wayne Grudem,** *1 Peter,* Tyndale New Testament Commentaries (Leicester, IVP, 1988), pp. 123–4.

Pastures, streams and valleys

He makes me lie down in green pastures; he leads me beside quiet
waters ... Even though I walk through the valley of the shadow of
death ...

What do you know about the geography of the land of Israel? To
understand this psalm you will need to do a little research here.
There are green pastures, quiet waters and dark ravines; is this a
description of what the land is always like? Israel and its environs are hot
and dry in the summer. Green pastures are few and far between. Jerusalem
has the same rainfall as London, but in half the number of days. When the
rains come in October or November they often begin with thunderstorms.
In heavy rain the water gushes down the mountainsides in torrents, leaving
deep gullies called wadis, which are dry and empty during the summer
months. These are unsuitable for sheep to drink from; they need oases, or
water drawn from a well, or slower moving streams or the quiet backwater
of a river. The point is that the shepherd knows where the pastures are, and
where the water is. He guides and provides; his care and thoughtfulness is
emphasized in verse two.

It is easy to apply these ideas to the LORD in his relations with those who
trust him. But perhaps there is contrast here, also. An ordinary shepherd
may be hard put to it to find green pastures and still waters. Was David
always able to bring his flock to places like this? In some summers pools
that were usually suitable might have dried up, pastures might have become
dusty fields of brown. By contrast with the human shepherd and the
experience of literal sheep, the LORD knows how to lead his people to
pastures green and refreshing water and to restore their souls.

Verse four gives a picture of a deep, dark and fearsome valley. Such
valleys are not infrequent in the mountainous area that makes up much of
Israel. They are places of danger and possible death. There are cliffs with
fearful drops; rough and rocky terrain which can lead to a sheep breaking a

leg. There are caves and dark corners where predators can lurk. To read about such places and perhaps see photographs gives a better idea of the picture here. The pilgrimage of God's people goes through a difficult and dangerous world, with lurking enemies, but it is the LORD who guides.

Mountains and valleys in the Bible

It is worth noting that features like mountains and valleys often seem to have a symbolic significance in the Bible, as well as a literal one; in some cases, of course, the significance is completely symbolic (see Psalm 2:6; Revelation 14:1). Jesus preached his famous sermon on a mount: probably on a level place on the side of a high hill. That is a literal fact, but there is clearly a symbolic link with Moses coming from Mount Sinai and bringing the law of God. The mountain there spoke of going up to the transcendent God who manifested his power and glory around its clefts and ridges. In Matthew's Gospel there is a new Moses, a greater than Moses, instructing a new people of God on what life is to be like in the kingdom of heaven. And just as Moses came down to find gross idolatry going on in the plain below, so when Jesus comes down he is immediately confronted with the effects of sin in the case of the unclean leper, the centurion's servant and the fever of Peter's mother-in-law.

Belief system

The LORD is my shepherd.

W ho is the LORD? What did David understand when he used this name? There is a belief system woven into this psalm. LORD is the covenant name of Israel's God. The Hebrew word is based on the 'name' God gave himself in Exodus 3:14, 'I AM WHO I AM'. He is the self-existent, eternal God. What he was, he always is and always will be. He has committed himself to his people. He has chosen them, made them his own, entered into covenant with them, given them promises. The sense of assurance and confidence which breathes in this psalm arises from an understanding of who the LORD is, and what he has done. The early books of the Old Testament, and the explanation of the name of God, were part of the heritage of the Israel to which David belonged. So if you want to know the spiritual background out of which his knowledge of God grew, and on which his faith was nurtured, you have to look at the Scriptures which David knew.

Three different expressions of belief

There are three different aspects to consider at this point. We've just looked at the first, what we might call the theological background, the ideas clustering round the word LORD. Secondly, you can trace out the beliefs which are explicitly expressed in this psalm, the truths which are taught, though not in this case in formal propositions but through the medium of the imagery. For example, the psalm shows that God is one who goes with his people, as the shepherd goes with the sheep. He is not remote, far off. His presence in the world is a reality to David. He is a God whose presence and grace is experienced by his people. The paths he chooses for his people are paths of righteousness, which implies that he is a righteous God. He leads them in this way for his name's sake—that is, because he is the kind of God he is.

Thirdly, a passage of Scripture may express an aspect of truth that has not been stated in that way before, and so it amplifies the truth, adding a new dimension to it. Or, as Scripture revelation develops historically a passage may go beyond what has previously been revealed. Hope beyond the grave is not always expressed clearly in the Old Testament, particularly in the earlier books, but here David affirms *and I will dwell in the house of the* LORD *for ever.* David is hardly saying that he expects to live in the earthly tabernacle for ever. Nor, in fact, could he actually live in the tabernacle at all. Not even the priests were permitted to do that. While it is true that the Hebrew does not necessarily mean what we mean by *for ever,* it is suggestive to notice the contrast between the two halves of verse 6. In particular, *for ever* contrasts with *all the days of my life*, so David is looking beyond the days of his life in the second clause. *The house of the* LORD suggests God's home, the place where his presence is; that's where David expects to dwell for ever.

Tracing out beliefs

In some cases it is difficult to understand the belief system, or theology, that lies behind, and is expressed in, a particular composition. This is the case with some whole books. Readers have often been puzzled, for example, by the book of Ecclesiastes. On the one hand it repeatedly echoes with the refrain, 'Vanity of vanities', or 'Meaningless, meaningless', while in other places it seems to speak quite differently (e.g. 2:24–26; 3:12,13). Part of the key is to notice how often the preacher speaks of life 'under the sun'. Seen from that perspective, looking at life just as it appears in this world, 'under the sun', all seems to be vain and transitory. But the other verses show us what the real situation is. Looking with the eyes of faith, everything is different. To get to the heart of the theology of the book it is those passages which speak of God that we need to consider.

The book of Esther doesn't mention the name of God at all, but it is not difficult to see the activity of God behind the events that the book recounts. The scene is set far from the land of Judah and the city of Jerusalem, in Susa, the capital of Persia. Here are some of God's people in a thoroughly pagan setting. This may be one reason why God's name is not mentioned, they lived in a land where the true God was unknown. Yet where God's name is not known he is very much present and active in caring for his own and working things together for their good. Part of the purpose of the book is to comfort and encourage those who, like us, live in godless environments.

The Song of Songs is another book from which God's name is absent. This book is full of imagery drawn from the natural world: vineyards, flocks of sheep, gardens, trees, stags, flowers, fruit and so on. The main characters are a man and a woman deeply in love. The setting reminds us of Genesis. God created everything and it was all very good. He made the first man and put him in a garden. He made the first woman from the side of the man, and brought her to him. The man was joined to the woman, becoming one flesh with her, and began to fulfil the commission to multiply and fill the earth. So the Song of Songs pictures human love as right and pure, part of the God-created order and thus good. It presents the ideal in a world that has been marred and spoilt by sin and the curse. It is true that many have understood the Song allegorically to depict the relationship between God and his people. But it can only function in that way if the original picture is one that is right, good and wholesome. Such is the beauty and power of the basic picture that even those who doubt that the book should be understood as an allegory are likely to go on to say as E. J. Young does:

The book may be regarded as a tacit parable. The eye of faith—as it beholds this picture of exalted human love—will be reminded of the one Love that is above all earthly and human affections—even the love of the Son of God for lost humanity.[1]

So be alert to the underlying theology of particular books, and remember that this is not simply expressed in sentences about God, but by image and illustration and in poetic form. A warm heart, prayerfully depending on the Holy Spirit's guidance, a thoughtful mind, and careful reading will yield rich rewards. Commentaries and other books can clearly give a great deal of help, but learn to use the methods they use, and not simply to accept their conclusions.

Reading the Old Testament
In looking at the Old Testament there are two different perspectives that must be borne in mind. In the first place you need to remember that truth has been revealed gradually through history—'at many times and in

various ways', as Hebrews 1:1 expresses it. God did not reveal all the truth about himself on one single occasion, but rather different aspects of his name, character and purposes have been revealed progressively. In particular the different facets of God's salvation, and the Saviour who will come to accomplish it, are unfolded throughout the Old Testament period in many different ways. The idea of the Messiah, or Christ, as King is prominent at the time of David and Solomon, but the picture of the suffering Servant of the Lord, though present in Psalm 22, comes to a clear expression much later in the prophecy of Isaiah. Do not overlook the wonderful way in which God revealed more and more of his purposes of goodness throughout the Old Testament.

But there is another perspective. You need to read the Old Testament in the light of its fulfilment and flowering in the New Testament. You will soon go wrong if you don't. When a shoot comes up in the garden and a bud develops, some of us may be at a loss to know exactly what to expect, but when the flower comes out we are entitled to interpret the bud in terms of what it turns out to be. So it is with the Old Testament. *The LORD is my shepherd.* The New Testament clearly identifies Jesus as the shepherd—the good shepherd, the great shepherd, the chief shepherd. So while it is possible for us to understand *shepherd* here of the Father, or the triune God, we are more likely to refer to the Son, our Lord Jesus Christ.

Progressive revelation

More ought to be said about the fact that God has revealed truth progressively, or cumulatively, throughout the history of Bible times. It is true that Abraham looked forward to the fulfilment of God's promises, and it is also true that in some way he foresaw the day when the Messiah would come (John 8:56). Yet Abraham could not have written John 3:16, 'For God so loved the world that he gave his one and only Son, that whoever believes in him shall not perish but have eternal life.' That verse belongs to the full light of New Testament times, when Jesus has actually come and has begun his ministry.

In addition we have to distinguish between objective revelation and the grasp which contemporaries might have had of that revelation. The disciples were very slow to grasp what Jesus taught them about his own death and resurrection. We have promises and prophecies concerning the events surrounding the return of Jesus Christ. Yet there are considerable differences among Christians in their understanding of these things. We shall only really see them in their rightful place when Christ returns and we can look back on all that has happened. If this is so, how much more difficult was it for those in the early days of the Old Testament era, as they tried to discover what the future held from the promises they had been given.

Let me also briefly comment on the difference between Psalm 22 and Isaiah 53 and the way in which Isaiah 53 develops the picture of the Messiah as the one who suffers for his people. Psalm 22 is written mainly as the experience of the psalmist. Doubtless it arose out of some extraordinarily deep and desolating experience that David passed through. His language and imagery went far beyond what had actually happened to him, so that it could express the agony of the Messiah on the cross. It is true that as the psalm progresses David fades into the background and it seems it is 'the afflicted one' (v .24) who takes the centre of the picture. Yet this is quite different from Isaiah 52:13–53:12. There, all the way through, the focus is on the one whom the Lord, speaking through the prophet, calls 'my servant'. In Psalm 22 no reasons are given for the sufferings, deep and terrible as they are. However, Isaiah makes it plain he 'took up our infirmities, and carried our sorrows' (53:4). The substitutionary nature of the sufferings is clearly expressed and, in measure, their accomplishments: 'He shall see the travail of his soul, and be satisfied. By his knowledge my righteous servant shall justify many, for he shall bear their iniquities' (53:11, New King James Version). There is considerable advancement in revealed truth about the sufferings of the Messiah in Isaiah, who came some 300 years after David.

Note

1 **E.J. Young,** *Introduction to the Old Testament* (London, Tyndale Press, 1956), p. 327.

The author

The LORD is MY shepherd.

Knowledge of an author and his life will usually enhance understanding of what he has written. Some of the books of the Bible are anonymous, for example, 1 and 2 Samuel and 1 and 2 Kings in the Old Testament, and Hebrews in the New Testament, but in many cases the author's name is given. Many of the psalms are attributed to David. The headings above each psalm are not strictly part of the text, and shouldn't be thought of as divinely inspired. Nevertheless they are very old and the New Testament confirms his authorship of a number of them, including two that are not attributed to him in the Psalter (Psalm 2 [Acts 4:25] and Psalm 95 [Hebrews 4:7]). There is no reason to doubt that these headings are reliable, and he probably wrote even more psalms that have no name attached to them

It is valuable to know who the author of this psalm is, because this one is particularly personal. All the way through it is 'I'. And though David began his psalm by speaking of God as 'he', when he comes to speak of the valley of the shadow of death he turns directly to God, 'you'. The tone is meditative and thoughtful. Here is a godly person reflecting on the way God has dealt with him, and what that means in terms of his present assurance and future hope.

David's experience

Clearly this psalm arises out of David's experience. Firstly, and most obviously, there is David's experience as a shepherd. Having cared for sheep himself, he knows how shepherd's care for their sheep. Possibly it was while he was watching over sheep that the thought first came to him of God acting as a shepherd towards him.

But if he had experience as a shepherd in a literal sense, he also had experience of being a sheep in a spiritual sense. Perhaps far better than most people, David would be able to compare himself to a sheep. He knew the ways of sheep, he understood what they were like, he knew what they needed. Perhaps a wry smile came across his face as he compared himself to some of the sheep that had proved themselves awkward and difficult, constantly needing his watchful eye on them.

He also had experience of shepherding people. It seems that God chose him to be king over Israel partly because of his experience as a shepherd— God wanted a shepherd king, not a self-centred tyrant. 'He chose David his servant, and took him from the sheep pens; from tending the sheep he brought him to be the shepherd of his people Jacob, of Israel his inheritance. And David shepherded them with integrity of heart; with skilful hands he led them' (Psalm 78:70–72). David not only knew how to manage sheep, but also how to rule and guide the people in his kingdom.

Beyond these things David had been brought through many varied experiences. We might think that his early days in Jesse's household were fairly carefree, for he would certainly be cut off from the main events that were taking place in Israel. Yet caring for sheep involved him in obvious personal danger when he tackled the lion and the bear. After that there came the time when he experienced increasing hostility from Saul and had to run for his life, when there was, as he put it, 'only a step between me and death' (1 Samuel 20:3). It was out of many dangers and God's protecting hand that he penned his psalm.

This raises an interesting question. When did David compose Psalm 23, at what time in his life? There is, of course, no certain way of determining this. The evidence suggests considerable experience of God's care, so it is likely that David wrote it after he had come to the throne. On the other hand, *Surely goodness and love will follow me all the days of my life*, does not suggest that he was close to the end of his days. As suggested, the basic thought of God caring for him as a shepherd might have come to him when he was caring for sheep himself. During the long periods out on his own watching over them, he had plenty of time to think and meditate. But he may have actually composed the psalm later on.

The Holy Spirit

Do not overlook the fact that the Holy Spirit enabled David to write. This is not simply a deduction from the fact that many of his psalms are preserved for us. In 2 Samuel 23:1–2 we read, 'These are the last words of David. "The oracle of David son of Jesse, the oracle of the man exalted by the Most High, the man anointed by the God of Jacob, Israel's singer of songs: "The Spirit of the LORD spoke through me; his word was on my tongue."' God not only raised David up to the throne, he also spoke through him by his Spirit, thus making him 'Israel's singer of songs'. Psalm 23 is not simply a deeply moving expression of David's own experience of God's care, it is a divinely given example of the care God has for all who put their trust in him.

Authors and their works

When we think about an author it is good to ask ourselves why they wrote what they did, and what purpose they hoped to fulfil through their writing. Reflection on both these points is helpful in trying to understand what they wrote. At the same time we are often dependent on the text itself for clues to the author's motivation in writing. This is generally the case with the letters of Paul, though the record in Acts can also be helpful. If we take 1 Corinthians as an example we find that at the beginning of chapter seven Paul says, 'Now for the matters you wrote about …'. It is quite evident from this that Paul is now beginning to respond to some questions, or, more likely, arguments, which the Corinthians had put to him. His repeated 'Now about …' (7:25; 8:1; 12:1) suggests that there were several points to which he had to reply. The problem is that we have his responses, but we do not know exactly what it was the Corinthians had said to him.

There are two dangers here. The first is that we may ignore the fact that Paul was responding to the Corinthians and treat what he is saying either as general teaching, or worse, that he is responding to *our* questions; in the case of chapter seven, *our* questions about marriage and divorce. The other danger is that a speculative reconstruction is drawn up of what the Corinthians were saying and this is then used to control the interpretation of what Paul has said. As it happens, in this case it seems possible to determine at least the main emphasis of the Corinthians' understanding— that marriage is probably wrong for Christians and is at least undesirable (see vv. 1–7 and vv. 10–11)—and to understand what Paul says against this background.

Some scholars have speculated about the purposes the writers of the Gospels had in penning their works, and they have ended up imagining certain settings in the early churches which the Gospels were written to deal with. This is not all entirely without foundation, but it is better to keep on firmer ground. John tells us he wrote his Gospel, 'that you may believe that Jesus is the Christ, the Son of God, and that by believing you may have life in his name' (John 20:31). The contents of the book bear this out, and it seems likely that the primary purpose of all four Gospels is evangelistic. What is important to note is that each Gospel is different, and each of them should therefore be understood on its own terms. Harmonies of the Gospels have their uses in trying to establish the overall chronology of the life of Jesus and the events which they record, but each Gospel writer presents his own portrait of Christ and uses his material in the way that fulfils his own purpose.

Literary conventions

A ny author naturally expresses himself according to the conventions of his own day. At any given time and in any given society there is a conventional way of speaking, and a conventional way of writing poetry. Think first of linguistic conventions: no two languages are the same. Translation is never simply a matter of replacing one set of words by another set of words. Word order varies from language to language. No translation represents the original completely adequately. This is why it can be useful to compare various translations. Hebrew uses constructions that differ from English constructions. So David expresses himself in ways that English people would not do. There are nuances to his language that only those who know Hebrew well are able to pick up. This is not very important in this psalm, because of its simplicity and clarity. However, *I shall not want* (Authorized Version), is not the way anyone is likely to express themselves today. So the NIV translation, *I shall not be in want*, or the words of the hymn, *I nothing lack*, help to clarify the meaning.

However, the Revised English Bible translation, *he revives my spirit*, gives a slightly different emphasis to *he restores my soul*. Are these to be thought of as alternatives? Is one more accurate than the other? The same question arises over the translation of *paths of righteousness*. Should this be, he leads me in right paths, that is, paths that are right for me, paths of his choosing? Or is it, as we usually think, paths that are characterized by righteousness, that is, the ways of holiness and goodness?

This raises another question. Do we always have to choose between alternatives like this? Might it be that what David has said is deliberately ambiguous? Poetry frequently exploits ambiguity and this is probably the case in both the above examples. This is the view, for example, of Derek Kidner, who says, 'In our context the two senses evidently interact.'[1] Nearly all of us are in the hands of experts when it comes to the original languages of the Bible. We should be aware that sometimes a word might have a broader or narrower sense than we would give to it in English, and that there might be places where two senses add to the overall meaning of the word or phrase.

Hebrew also has different poetic conventions. In the second section we will look more closely at Hebrew poetry, but it is quite clear that the psalms are different from the forms of traditional English poetry. Each language also has different idioms. Idioms are language forms characteristic of a particular language, but not generally repeatable in another language. *Quiet waters* is literally *waters of resting places*. This is not the way people speak or write in English, and it raises a question about the precise meaning. Is the sense: waters that are at rest? Or does it mean: waters that sheep can rest by? Or is it perhaps, thinking of the previous paragraph, that sheep rest beside quiet waters? At this point it is worth considering how 'waters of rest' relates to *green pastures*. If *green pastures* suggests food for the sheep (as well as rest, *lie down*), then *waters* probably refers primarily to drinking and so *quiet waters* would be the most appropriate translation.

Further reflections on conventions

The question of ambiguity is a difficult one. On the one hand, while words may have a broad range of meaning, they generally take their specific meaning from the context in which they occur. In such a case it would be quite wrong to enlarge the meaning of the word to include another possible shade of meaning that does not emerge from the context—'getting a blessing both ways', as it is sometimes called. On the other hand it is not just poetry that exploits ambiguity. John in his Gospel frequently uses words that are capable of being understood in more than one way, and this seems certain to be intentional. One of the most well-known examples occurs in chapter three, where 'born again' can also mean 'born from above'. In fact the Greek word *logos*, 'word', which is found in the opening verses has several meanings, and makes the Gospel accessible to readers from diverse backgrounds.

One writer suggested the same might be true in 2 Corinthians 3:18, 'And we, who with unveiled faces all reflect the Lord's glory, are being transformed into his likeness ...'. In this verse the NIV uses the word 'reflect' in the text, but has the word 'contemplate' in the margin, which is similar to the NKJV's 'beholding'. 'Perhaps,' he wrote, 'Paul intended both senses, "to reflect by beholding".' Although I think 'behold, contemplate' is the primary meaning, yet in the context Moses both beheld something of the glory of the Lord and reflected it in his face (Exodus 33:21–23; 34:5–7, 29–35). In the end it has to be the context which is the determining factor. Often the context limits the meaning of a word, but not always.

Note

1 **Derek Kidner,** *Psalms 1–72,* Tyndale Old Testament Commentaries (London, IVP, 1973) p. 110.

Customs

You anoint my head with oil.

Customs differ according to country and time. There were certainly customs in Bible times that are different from ours today. And as 'Bible times' covers some 1,500 years and several different countries, there are a variety of differing customs in the Bible. And, of course, they can differ within a country. In verse 5 David says, *You anoint my head with oil.* To what is he referring? This partly depends on other considerations. Does the picture change in verse 5? Are we intended to pursue the image of the sheep with their shepherd, or are we now thinking about David brought in to a feast? In view of the words *table, cup* and *house,* as well as this particular phrase, it is almost certain that the picture changes here. This is unlikely to be a shepherd applying oil to the head of a sheep, which would presumably be medicinal. Rather, this is the realm of hospitality, as in Luke 7:46, 'You did not put oil on my head…' (compare also Psalm 141:5). This is certainly not something that people in western countries do when welcoming their guests. What was its purpose? The whole picture seems to be one of a joyful banquet—note the overflowing cup. The anointing was a sign of welcome and respect and was possibly also perfumed, which was helpful as conditions were smelly in those days. At the practical level it served to freshen the face in dry and dusty days, but the main emphasis is on a joyful welcome as an honoured guest.

How would the psalm have been received, understood and used by its first readers and hearers? Interpreters have to try and think themselves into the minds of the people of those days. It is *their* understanding of the shepherd, *their* understanding of verse 5 that we want to try and get hold of. This very easily leads on to the world in front of the text, which is the subject of Part 3.

Customs beyond Psalm 23

Quite clearly the Bible refers to customs which are different from the customs of the Western world in the twenty-first century. It is important to try to understand the significance of customs. Sometimes they seem strange to us, sometimes we don't realize the differences between some biblical customs and our customs. There is no necessary reason why customs that had a particular significance then should be repeated today, when they may have no such significance, or perhaps even a different one, simply because they are in the Bible. In several of the Epistles Christians are told to greet each other with a holy kiss. This was part of Jewish culture, and may have been primarily men with men and women with women. It was a greeting, probably with a kiss on both cheeks, and did not have the same sort of significance which has generally been given to a kiss in western culture.

God

This section, *The world behind the text*, could have begun by considering that Psalm 23 is part of the Bible, and therefore part of God's Word. As it was, it began with the picture of the shepherd because that is so striking in the opening verses. However, it is important to realize the significance of the psalm's place in Scripture. We touched on this when remembering that David was the sweet psalmist of Israel through whom the Holy Spirit spoke. Ultimately, behind the text of the Bible stands the living God. He is a God who communicates with men and women. In the early days he spoke directly to Adam and Eve, to Noah and to others. He also employed dreams and visions, though using speech as well, to convey the message he had for them. Then he used spokesmen, prophets, rather than direct speech. At this point we begin to enter a realm which is beyond the understanding of any of us. In what way did God give to the prophets what he wanted spoken? How far did he use the processes of the human mind with its cultural conditioning to deliver what he had to say? On a few occasions prophets may have acted more as reporters—the Ten Commandments may be a case in point—but quite clearly this is not so with most of the biblical literature. In a highly personal poem like this, David was fully active in reflecting on his experience and composing a concise masterpiece. It is truly David's work. Yet it is also the Word of God.

Supremely in the 'world behind the text' is God himself. It is his purpose to communicate all he desires to say to the human race. Though this was through oral revelation at one time, now all we need has been written down. The Holy Spirit superintended all the writing of Scripture, so that what we have is truly the work of men, yet also surely the Word of God. God has used the creativity and capability of his own creatures to make his ways and will known to them all. It is probably correct to think that the human mind has never been so intensively active as in the production of the Bible. In the writings of Paul we may be seeing intellectual brilliance of a kind that shines nowhere else. In Isaiah we have visionary thought at its most exalted, and in the Psalms the deepest and most accurate descriptions of the emotional and spiritual sensitivities that people are capable of.

Certain things follow from this. The ultimate author of Scripture is God, so what we need to know is what he has to say to us. He says it through the words of his servants, so as we understand them, we are also understanding him. At the same time it is possible that there is more to their words than they themselves were capable of realizing at the time (see 1 Peter 1:10–12). That is to say, what they wrote takes on an enlarged and more Christ-oriented meaning in the light of the coming of Jesus Christ and the New Testament revelation.

This point needs careful thought, and some distinctions should be made. In the light of the New Testament it is appropriate to see Jesus Christ as our divine shepherd. He is God; the term LORD is given to him in the New Testament, and he has been especially appointed by the Father to shepherd the sheep (see John 10, for example). This is not, however, to say that David understood this, or that he had clear insight into the triune nature of God—though Psalm 110:1 and 34:7 show that he used language which points in that direction.

To take a further step: would it be possible to think of this psalm as expressing the sentiments of Jesus as David's son? Perhaps it would in the sense that Jesus was the 'sheep' par excellence, the one who fully trusted God and passed through the valley of the shadow of death at its worst. Yet this would simply be *applying* the psalm to Jesus. It would certainly be mistaken to see this psalm as foreshadowing Jesus as the Lamb of God, with all the sacrificial associations of that phrase.

God, the ultimate author

Behind the text of Scripture, then, we have a gracious God who speaks his Word to us through his servants. Our supreme task is to discern rightly what he is saying to us. For this we need reverence, humility, prayerfulness and honesty before a text which has such significance for us.

I once heard a missionary, preaching at a service at which a young man was being set apart for service abroad, tell us that Paul wrote his letters by inspiration, but today's missionaries had to write their prayer letters without any such assistance! Therefore, he concluded, don't be surprised if, in the middle of busy schedules, missionaries don't write as many letters as you would like. Of course he was being humorous—though the point about missionaries being busy people was a valid one. But he was wrong to imply that writing under inspiration necessarily made it any easier. In fact Paul and the other biblical writers used their own minds, researched their own material where necessary (see Luke 1:1–4), and wrote out of their own experience. So we cannot expect that interpreting the Bible is likely to be any easier a discipline. The Holy Spirit who impelled and guided the endeavours of the biblical writers will help us as we depend prayerfully on him in seeking to understand the Bible, but this will not take place without careful thought and hard work.

Review and further study

1. Don't jump to conclusions about what a Bible passage means. Read it carefully. What is the writer actually saying? Look at other passages which might throw light on it. Use other books which may throw light on the background of the passage. What is the main thrust and emphasis of the writer here? Beware of extending the meaning in directions that go away from that. Do not only notice comparisons, note the contrasts as well.

2. Consider what the passage reveals of the author's beliefs. What undergirding truths can you discern? Does he bring out truth in a new way here?

3. In looking at the Old Testament ask yourself what the text meant to the author and the people of his day. Are there ways in which this relates to truths that are developed in a fuller way in the New Testament? What relation does this passage have to the overall theme of the Bible and God's provision of a Saviour?

4. What do you know of the author of a passage? Does this knowledge help in understanding the text? Does the passage, or its context, give you an insight into his purpose(s) in writing?

5. Does the passage use expressions that seem strange to those who use the English language? Is it possible to see what is intended by these and to understand them in a more 'English' way? Are there customs that do not belong to our culture? Even if the passage seems very unrelated to life today are there valid principles which we can use?

6. Scripture's ultimate author is God; what attitudes of mind and heart

are appropriate for those who read his Word? While there is much in the Bible that is plain and clear, especially the way of salvation, we must expect to give careful thought and engage in serious research if we want to understand it as fully as possible.

To think about or discuss

Psalm 90 was written by Moses; what light does Moses' life and leadership of Israel throw on this psalm?

What beliefs are explicit or implicit in that psalm?

Part II
The world within the text

Having looked behind the text of Psalm 23 our next step is to look at what it actually says. Even if we knew nothing about David or about the background of the days when he lived, we could still learn a great deal from the psalm itself. The background helps, but the actual words of the psalm are crucial.

The previous chapter finished with the reminder that the most important factor behind the text is God himself, for he is the ultimate author of Scripture. The Bible is his Word, as well as the words of the human authors of the different books. It was the Holy Spirit, in particular, who worked in and through the minds of the human authors who penned the pages of the Bible. In the Bible we hear the voice of the Holy Spirit. Some verses in the letter to the Hebrews are especially helpful in considering this. Chapter three and verse seven of Hebrews begins like this, 'So, as the Holy Spirit says, "Today, if you hear his voice, do not harden your hearts …".' This is the beginning of a long quotation from Palm 95. But it is the Holy Spirit who speaks what the psalm is saying. Hebrews 9:8 speaks of the fact that the high priest entered the most holy part of the tabernacle only once a year and goes on to say, 'The Holy Spirit indicating this …' (NKJV). And chapter ten, verse fifteen reads, 'The Holy Spirit also testifies to us about this', and follows with a quotation from Jeremiah 31. In these three places Hebrews attributes the Old Testament to the Holy Spirit.

What is most interesting, however, is that in each case the verb is in the present tense—'says', 'indicating', 'testifies'. In other words the Holy Spirit is still speaking through Scripture. Whether a person hardens his heart or listens intently, it is the Spirit who speaks the words of Psalm 23 as much as Psalm 95. So the question we have to ask ourselves is this, how should a person listen when the Holy Spirit is speaking?

If God were actually present with us we would listen attentively to what he had to say. We would listen carefully, so as to make sure we didn't miss or misinterpret anything he said to us. We would listen humbly and reverently. We would be so thankful that God was speaking, because we know that what God says is important and true. These should be our attitudes when we listen to Scripture because it is the voice of the Spirit to us. Isaiah 66:2 says, 'This is the one I esteem: he who is humble and contrite in spirit, and trembles at my word.' And Ezekiel tells of his own experience: 'Then he said to me, "Son of man, eat this scroll I am giving you and fill your stomach with it". So I ate it, and it tasted as sweet as honey in my mouth' (Ezekiel 3:3). We should tremble before the Word of God, yet at the same time rejoice at its sweetness and the spiritual enlightenment and strengthening that it gives.

Literary form

If we look at the text of Psalm 23 the most obvious feature is that it is a poem. Even if it were not set out as poetry, as it is in modern versions of the Bible, its poetic structure is very clear. In identifying it as poetry we are commenting on its literary form or, to use the technical word, its genre. We must always read a piece of writing according to its form. In many cases we do this automatically because we are accustomed to different forms of writing, but in the Bible, where some of the forms are not so much used today, it is necessary to make sure we know what it is we are reading. There are, for example, obvious differences between parable and narrative, between proverb and law.

Once we have identified a genre, or literary form, this creates an expectation of how the writing is going to proceed. In some cases the very first words may alert us to what it is we are reading. If we start reading a text and it begins, 'Once upon a time …', then we expect a fairy story. If it begins, 'I leave all my estate …', then we realize that it is a will. In the Bible it is generally not as simple as that, but the Letters begin with a conventional greeting except in the case of Hebrews and 1 John. Luke begins his Gospel and Acts with prologues that follow some of the current conventions of history writing. The general principle is to familiarize ourselves as much as we can with the different forms in the Bible so that we read each part appropriately. There are, for example, broad genres. In addition to narrative, poetry and law we could add gospel, letter, prophecy and apocalyptic—think of the book of Revelation for this last category. Then there are smaller generic units. In addition to proverb and parable some of the most easily recognizable are genealogy, doxology and benediction.

In his book, *How Literature Works*, Kenneth Quinn, a secular author commenting on writing in general, says something that is important for readers of the Bible to recognize. 'The fact remains that reading a novel or a poem … is a different kind of experience from reading other texts (a news item in a newspaper, an article in an encyclopaedia, the minutes of a meeting).'[1] Quinn is trying to distinguish between literature—novels and poetry—and other forms of writing. Though it is not always easy to draw hard and fast lines there is little doubt that he is correct in what he says.

Behind literature lies the oral stage. Writing has been going on right back since before the time of Moses, but at first it was a slow and laborious practice on clay tablets. Only a few could write, and only a few could read. But everyone could speak, and all could listen. So the role of storyteller arose. The stories of the family, and the tribe and then the nation would be passed on. People learnt to tell the past in interesting ways, holding the attention of their audience. It was possible to invent stories, also to compose songs to sing together, and to put words together in short, snappy ways, using rhythm, alliteration or word play, enabling people to remember them and use them again. It was out of this oral use of words that literature was born, and a great deal of the Bible reflects this background.

The sort of writing that we are most used to came much later, being influenced by the need to pass on information, whether news or scientific discovery. So a type of factual, descriptive writing arose which we might call utilitarian prose. We have it today in newspapers and school and college textbooks. This is the staple reading of most of us and does not prepare us for reading the Bible which, generally speaking, is much more literary in form, as we shall see when we consider its poetry and narrative.

So we have to make a conscious effort when it comes to Bible reading. To quote from Quinn again: 'The way we read a poem or a novel differs from the way we read an article in a newspaper or an encyclopaedia. We prepare ourselves to think harder, more imaginatively—more responsively… reading the newspaper, reading letters—these are things we do all the time, they're as easy and natural as walking … Reading a poem or a novel is like swimming: it's an activity that has to be learnt ...'.[2] That is partly why this book has been written. Of course many Christians are already very familiar with the Psalms, so they have gained at least some experience in reading biblical poetry. But parts of the Bible are more difficult for us, and it takes perseverance and practice to get the most out of them.

Poetry

Psalm 23 is a poem. What exactly is a poem? How does a poem differ from a piece of prose writing? There is no precise dividing line: it is possible to have lyrical prose. The New Testament has little actual poetry, but it does have lyrical prose, 1 Corinthians 13, for example. Coleridge described poetry as 'The best words in the best order'—the best words, the most suitable, the most telling, in the best order. A dictionary definition says, 'Poem: a composition in verse, usually characterised by concentrated and heightened language in which words are chosen for their sound and suggestive power as well as for their sense, and using such techniques as metre, rhyme and alliteration.'[3] The form of a poem is important. It makes an impact not simply by what it says, but by the way it says it. The appeal of a poem does not arise from the logic of the words, or the skill of argumentation of the writer, but from its beauty and its artistry. A poem is not to be read literally, nor should you expect consistency in a poem. Psalm 23 shifts from one picture to another in moving from verse 4 to verse 5. A poem often has an immediate appeal, and yet at the same time repays reflection and thought. It may present images which open up wider thoughts as you ponder what it says.

So what is the benefit of a poem? A poem suits reflection. It is a piece of writing to think over, to meditate upon. A poem aids communication. It communicates truth in words of force and feeling and beauty. How much better it is to read the opening words of Psalm 23 than to have the same truth put in a matter of fact, prosaic form: 'The Lord acts towards me as a shepherd does towards his sheep. This means I shall not lack anything. He provides rest for me, and the food I need and water ...'. Already you can see that you lose a tremendous amount if you try to turn the picture of those verses into ordinary prose.

A poem aids memorization. What it says sticks in the mind. There are still many people who know Psalm 23 off by heart, not because they ever set themselves to learn it, but because they have often read it and it has made its own impact on their memory. The mind is more than the intellect, and poetry engages us more fully than most other forms of writing. A poem appeals to the imagination and stirs the emotions. It expresses the emotion of the poet in suitable words and evokes the emotional response of the reader. A poem like this one can wonderfully reassure. You can speak to Christians who are feeling troubled and distressed and assure them of truths which should encourage and help them. Yet this might fail to be of much help. Read this psalm to them and its effect is likely to be far more powerful. The very form soothes and all sorts of associations and ideas are sparked off in the mind.

Unfortunately many people don't read poetry today. This means that the poetic parts of the Bible are more difficult for twenty-first century people to understand. This is a great loss. Not so much, perhaps, with the book of Psalms because Christians tend to be familiar with most of them. However, much of prophecy is written in poetic form, as also a book like Job. One of the reasons many struggle with prophecy is because they don't know how to understand the poetic language which it uses.

Of course, what we have in the Bible is Hebrew poetry and this differs in several ways from traditional English poetry. The poetry we are used to depends very much on rhythm and rhyme, features which are found much less in the Hebrew form. In spite of that, reading poetry in English does help to condition the mind to poetic expression.

Notes

1 **Kenneth Quinn,** How Literature Works (Basingstoke, Macmillan, 1992), p. 1.
2 Ibid., p. 10.
3 Collins English Dictionary (London, Collins, 1985).

Hebrew poetry

There are four features of Hebrew poetry which we shall notice. This is only a very brief introduction and naturally deals with those features that carry over into English.

Parallelism

This is a very obvious feature of Hebrew poetry and has sometimes been described as its leading characteristic. Speaking generally it works like this. Two lines of poetry form a couplet, and the thought in the second line parallels that in the first in some way. Verse two is the most clear example in Psalm 23:

He makes me lie down in green pastures,
he leads me beside quiet waters.

This is an example of what used to be called synonymous parallelism, in which the second line says the same thing as the first line in slightly different words. It is now generally agreed that the thought is probably never exactly the same, there is always some difference which enhances the meaning and adds colour and interest to the couplet. You can see that this is so here. Another example of this type of parallelism comes in Psalm 24:3:

Who may ascend the hill of the LORD?
Who may stand in his holy place?

Here there is a much closer parallelism of thought, but even so there is a measure of progression which adds to the basic thought of who is fit to come before God. It is one thing to *ascend the hill of the LORD*; it is another to *stand in his holy place.*

Let me add that I have used the words 'line' and 'couplet' (i.e. two lines that belong together) for ease of understanding, but they are not the technical words that would be used in a textbook on Hebrew poetry.

Another type of parallelism has been called antithetic parallelism because there is a contrast between what is stated in the first line and what is stated in the second:

Righteousness exalts a nation,
but sin is a disgrace to any people (Proverbs 14:34).

A third type (synthetic parallelism) consists of a couplet in which the second line completes the thought. For this we return to Psalm 23 and verse 5:

You prepare a table before me
in the presence of my enemies.

The last type to be mentioned is often known as climactic parallelism. You only have to look at an example or two to see why it is given this name. In this case (as in others) the parallelism is not always restricted to two lines:

The seas have lifted up, O LORD,
the seas have lifted up their voice;
the seas have lifted up their pounding waves (Psalm 93:3).

Ascribe to the LORD, O families of nations,
ascribe to the LORD glory and strength.
Ascribe to the LORD the glory due to his name;
bring an offering and come into his courts (Psalm 96:7–8).

Parallelism is simply one way in which Hebrew poetry expresses thoughts in striking and memorable ways. Although it is valuable to isolate the different types of parallelism we do not need to do this to respond to its artistry. It works in a similar way to the way having two eyes enhances our sight. It gives depth of vision and perspective. By its repetition and symmetry, parallelism reinforces truth.

Imagery
Another way in which Hebrew poetry makes its appeal to those who read it

is by its use of imagery. This may be more important than parallelism. This psalm is full of images, as we have already seen. Even for modern city-dwellers it is easy to follow most of the images which are brought before us:

Even though I walk
through the valley of the shadow of death,
I will fear no evil,
for you are with me;
your rod and your staff,
they comfort me.

This use of imagery has certain consequences. It means first of all that we must not try to understand the psalm literally. The psalm mentions a shepherd, green pastures, quiet waters, a dark valley, a rod and staff, a table, oil and a cup, but it is about none of these things. None of them is actual; we are to look beyond all these images to the spiritual realities of the relationship those who trust in the Lord have with him. Poetry is like that; it deals in images:

O, my luve's like a red, red rose,
    That's newly sprung in June;
O, my luve's like the melodie,
    That's sweetly played in tune. (Robert Burns)

It means secondly that we cannot always identify precisely what the image refers to. David doesn't tell us exactly what *He makes me lie down in green pastures* refers to. There is an element of uncertainty here. On the one hand there is probably an immediate impression, on the other it makes us think. What does Burns mean by, 'O my luve's like a red, red rose'? Is he talking about the one he loves, or the love he has for her? Assuming it's the first does he mean she has red hair, or a red face, or that he is picturing her wearing red clothes? Almost certainly, he intends none of these things. He is thinking of the freshness, the beauty, the allure of a rose that has just opened. It is in its prime, it is at its best, it is irresistible. We have to realize this is true of biblical poetry too.

The desert and the parched land will be glad;
the wilderness will rejoice and blossom.
Like the crocus, it will burst into bloom (Isaiah 35:1).

Is Isaiah actually talking about deserts and the wilderness? Do landscapes have emotional lives?

'The days are coming,' declares the LORD,
'when the reaper will be overtaken by the ploughman
and the planter by the one treading grapes.
New wine will drip from the mountains
and flow from all the hills' (Amos 9:13).

This sounds wonderful, but it is not so easy to determine what it actually refers to.

Thirdly, then, imagery is often elusive and allusive. It is elusive in that though it gives you a general picture, as Amos does, it is often difficult to put your finger on precisely how it is to be understood. It is allusive because it often conjures up other pictures suggested by the same words. *Quiet waters*, for example, might lead a person to think of the time when the heavy rains were over, when torrents and floods were past and peace and tranquillity had taken their place. From the perspective of a Christian they might recall Jesus stilling the storm, the good Shepherd of his disciples calming the winds and waves with his 'Peace, be still'. This much later event would then provide an example of the Shepherd leading beside quiet waters.

Another example of allusion can be seen in one of Charles Wesley's hymns celebrating the birth of Jesus:

Our God contracted to a span,
Incomprehensibly made man.

Here 'a span' refers to God being born as a baby, no longer than the span of a man's hand—with a little poetic licence! But it is extremely likely that Wesley here borrows a phrase from George Herbert's poem 'The Pulley':

When God at first made man,
Having a glass of blessings standing by,
'Let us,' said he, 'pour on him all we can:
Let the world's riches, which dispersed lie,
   Contract into a span.'

Here there is the same thought of blessings being brought into a small space, but also of God pouring these blessings on to people. This suggests another meaning of span, spanning the distance between God and people. So perhaps Wesley is not just thinking of the size of the baby, but also that he is the bridge, the span, between 'Our God' and humankind. And even if Wesley didn't think it, it is true!

Fourthly, using imagery as Psalm 23 does invites the reader to supply the meaning. Verse two asks the reader to consider how lying down in green pastures and being led beside quiet waters apply in spiritual experience. That doesn't mean that we can supply any meaning we like. We have to be guided by the words David used and what we know of his background and experience. But it does mean that different readers are likely to focus on different aspects of the picture. Show a painting to different people and though their overall impression might be much the same, it is very likely that they will be attracted by different features. There is nothing wrong with that, it is the nature of pictures, and images, to prompt different reactions. This is one of the differences between legal writing, which has to be very precise and definitive, and poetry.

How then should imagery be read? First of all with an openness to what it is saying. This is so with every text, but it is particularly important to allow a poem to speak to you. Poetry is not as clear and straightforward as narrative, or as logical argumentation, or legal precision. First impressions are often important. You look at a picture, or a scene—on the sea coast, in a mountainous area—and it makes an impression. It fills you with awe, it makes you feel small, fear grips your heart, it makes you glad to be alive, you are overwhelmed with its beauty, your spirit surges with joy. So it is with imagery.

Secondly, imagery must be read with imagination. Imagery appeals to our imagination. This does not mean we should let our imagination run riot. There can be a danger, especially with narrative, of people imagining all sorts of detail that are not in the text of the Bible at all. But nevertheless, imagery—and narrative, for that matter—do appeal to the imagination. We are to *see* the shepherd and the sheep; to *imagine* ourselves with them going through the dark valley. It is in this way that we begin to make connections with the spiritual experience of which the image speaks.

Thirdly, read without making too precise identifications of the images with particular realities. Do *green pastures* equal the Scriptures? No. It is true that sheep feed and are nourished in green pastures. It is also true that the Shepherd nourishes our souls and that he does so through the Scriptures, but the picture is general, not precise. In the course of application the Scriptures can be mentioned, but that is a different matter. Is *You anoint my head with oil* a reference to the Holy Spirit? No. It is a picture of a person being welcomed as an honoured guest to a feast and it has a spiritual application, but there is no reference to the Holy Spirit in the image nor in the application either. We are being given a general picture. It is true that we fill that out as we consider all that is involved in it and suggested by it, but we should not make precise identifications. That is to turn imagery into allegory.

One further feature of imagery can be mentioned. In poetry images can often change quickly. This psalm has the extended image of the shepherd with his sheep, but that suddenly changes in verse five. Some try to carry the one image on into that verse, but that makes a clear and obvious picture suddenly take a very unusual turn and use language which seems unlikely to refer to sheep. One of the beauties of poetry is that it often moves from one picture to another like walking through an art gallery. The thing to do is to see the new image and consider it on its own terms. It may picture the same spiritual truth, but a new image brings out a new aspect. This is how some people view verse two—two pictures of rest, each adding to the other. In other cases it may be quite a different image, like that of the host who prepares a table in verse five, but still picturing the relationship between the Lord and a believer.

Metaphor

A metaphor is different from a simile. When Burns writes, 'O my luve's like a red, red rose' he is using a simile. He uses the word 'like'. When David writes, 'The LORD is my shepherd' he is using a metaphor. Although he means, 'The LORD is like a shepherd', that's not what he says. To say, 'The LORD is my shepherd' gives a greater sense of immediacy, than to use the word 'like'. Sheep have a shepherd; someone who cares for them and leads them. I have a Shepherd; the Lord who cares for me and leads me. A metaphor can be defined in a precise way: 'A figure of speech in which a word or phrase is applied to an object or action that it does not literally denote in order to imply a resemblance.'[1] Often, however, metaphor is used in a much broader way, and refers to figurative language. One recent definition of metaphor explains it like this, 'The essence of metaphor is understanding and experiencing one kind of thing in terms of another.'[2] Defined like that, the Bible is full of metaphors.

Everyday language is also full of metaphors. We might say that it is *peppered* with them; or *littered* with them. If it is raining heavily we say it is *pouring*, or even *raining cats and dogs*. A bad driver is a *road-hog*; a slow driver *crawls along*. When I suddenly find I can't write another sentence I have *writer's block*, and if I'm running a marathon I might well *hit the wall*. A terrible journey home might *be through hell and high water*, and once we're back and the front door is closed we feel *safe as houses*.

Some of these metaphors would make no sense to someone who speaks another language, even if he or she had some basic knowledge of English. Metaphors are often idiomatic, that is, they belong particularly to a language and culture and cannot be translated literally into another language, because they make no sense in that language. The book by Sandy gives some interesting examples of French metaphors literally translated into English. 'She gave him a rabbit', 'he has a cockroach', 'he saw thirty-six candles', give us no idea of what a Frenchman might mean by such phrases. This means we have to be careful when translating biblical metaphors, or when we try to understand language which is metaphorical and which does not sound an English way of putting things.

We can say that there are two kinds of metaphors. There are conventional metaphors; that is, metaphors that are used and understood generally by a particular group of people; the sort of metaphors given in the previous paragraph but one. But there are also what might be called literary metaphors, that is metaphors writers create to enable them to express the point they wish to make. David may have been one of the first to picture the Lord as a shepherd (there is an earlier reference in Genesis 49:24). After his time this seems to have become an accepted metaphor for the Lord as the one who cares for his people (see Psalm 80:1; Isaiah 40:11; Ezekiel 34:11ff). On the other hand when we read in Psalm 22:14, 'I am poured out like water' this seems to be a literary metaphor for the feeling of all strength and energy, as we would say, *ebbing away*. But it is more startling than the picture of the tide going out, vitality, energy, is *poured out like water*.

This raises two related questions. How do we spot and interpret what I have chosen to call literary metaphors? And how can we distinguish metaphors from what is intended to be literal? The answer to the first question is that we have to be alert to the possibility of metaphor, especially in poetry and (in the Bible) in prophecy. Interpreting, or understanding, metaphor comes by experience and reflection. Usually we can grasp what the writer is intending when we think about it. Answering the second question is not always easy. Psalm 22:14 goes on like this:

I am poured out like water,
and all my bones are out of joint.

If we understand this psalm to apply ultimately to the Messiah then the second clause seems to be literally true of the crucifixion of Jesus. (True, not *all* the bones of someone crucified would be out of joint, but it is likely that the sufferer would experience a feeling of agonizing dislocation). Psalm 22 is interesting in this connection because there is a mixture of metaphor and what was literally true of Jesus, as the New Testament makes clear (John 19:24). However, everyday speech is often mixed in this way. When we come across this in a text we have to read it carefully. Usually we will be able to distinguish between the metaphorical and literal.

Why do we use metaphors? Metaphors make the way we speak or write much more interesting. They make language vivid. Usually they add a picture to a concept. A fascinating example occurs in Matthew 27:44, 'The robbers who were crucified with him also heaped insults on him.' The

Greek uses one word which means: insult, reproach, revile, reprimand. But the NIV adds a metaphor, '*heaped* insults on him', making it much more vivid than simply 'insulted him'. The AV is even more surprising, 'The thieves also, which were crucified with him, *cast the same in his teeth.*' Five words where the original has one, and a wholly English metaphor to replace a straightforward Greek verb. Not precise translation, but it is a striking and appropriate phrase.

We find our Lord often using metaphors: 'No-one can *see* the *kingdom* of God unless he is *born again*'; 'I am the *way* and the *truth* and the *life*'; 'Blessed are those who *hunger and thirst* for righteousness'; 'Ask and it shall be given to you; seek and you will find; *knock* and *it shall be opened* to you'; 'Small is the *gate* and narrow the *road* that leads to life, and only a few find it.'

We might call Psalm 23:1–4 an extended metaphor, with another in v.5. Looking at it word by word we can see that shepherd, pastures, waters, paths, valley, rod, staff, table, oil, cup and house are all metaphors. In a poem like this there is little difference between 'metaphor' and 'imagery'. But individual metaphors can be more difficult to spot and understand. For example Psalm 58:6 says, 'Break the teeth in their mouths, O God; tear out, O LORD, the fangs of the lions!' In the context the opening words are a prayer referring to David's enemies. Is David actually asking that God will smash his foes in the mouth, breaking their teeth? No; of course not. The second half of the verse shows us that David is picturing his enemies as lions, and is praying that God will render the weapons of his enemies inoperative. Who fears a toothless lion?

Some psalms, like Psalm 91, have a succession of metaphors, each metaphor presenting a different picture. In Psalm 91:3, 'Surely he will save you from the fowler's snare', the believer is pictured as a bird whom God delivers from his enemy, who is pictured as a 'fowler', one who catches and sells birds. In the next verse the picture of a bird is resumed, but this time God is the mother bird who hides her chicks under her wings and keeps them safe. This is followed by the same idea of safety, but two other images are used, a shield and rampart—or, perhaps, buckler, another sort of shield.

Artistry

The fourth feature of Hebrew poetry is artistry, which is a feature of all poetry.

A poem is a work of art—the best words in the best order. Sometimes Christians focus too much on individual verses without getting the sense and scope of a whole passage. A poem needs to be looked at first of all as a whole, and then one can consider its parts more closely. A poem is generally beautiful, though this depends on its subject matter. It is memorable. It is both expressive and evocative. That is to say, it expresses the thoughts, desires, emotions, longings and meditations of the poet. But it also enables the reader to express similar desires and emotions and evokes a response from him or her. This is especially true of the Psalms. Again and again they prove to be vehicles for readers, even centuries later, to clarify and express their own spiritual longings. A psalm gives insight and understanding. It unlocks the heart and moves the soul. Human and divine artistry combine in the deepest, fullest, most suitable and beautiful of all collections of songs of devotion.

It is in large part because Psalm 23 is a psalm, a poem, that it has been the source of immeasurable comfort and assurance through the centuries. An uncle of mine, a conscientious objector at the time of the Second World War, became a paratrooper with the Royal Army Medical Corps. This is what he wrote about flying over to Normandy on D-Day:

Saw coast of England disappear. Shortly after saw navy & seaborne forces on way. Strong fighter escort protecting us. (No armaments on C.47a, except holes in windows for rifles, etc.) I ate glucose sweets & repeated to myself various texts. Found great strength in 23rd Psalm, particularly 'Yea, though I walk through the valley of the shadow of death, I will fear no evil, *for thou art with me'* & 'In quietness & in confidence shall be your strength.' Felt perfectly calm & natural.—Never felt anything like it at any time while flying, not even when there's been no jump to look forward to!

There is one other feature of Hebrew poetry which can only be appreciated in a very limited way in translation. This is word-play. That the book of Psalms makes fairly considerable use of this can be seen in the acrostic psalms. The most obvious from the point of view of an English reader is Psalm 119. This psalm is divided into twenty-two sections, the number of the letters of the Hebrew alphabet. Each section has a letter printed before it, and every one of the eight verses in the section begins with a word that begins with the appropriate letter. This indicates that the psalmist took a great deal of time and trouble to compose his psalm. There are other psalms—Psalm 34 is one—in which each verse begins with a different letter going through the alphabet. It is not at all easy to do this in English. Timothy Dudley-Smith has done excellent acrostic versions of Psalm 34 and Psalm 25. The first verse of Psalm 25 in his version goes like this:

All my soul to God I raise;
Be my guardian all my days.
Confident in hope I rest,
Daily prove your path is best.
Ever work in me your will,
Faithful to your promise still.

(Copyright Timothy Dudley-Smith; used by permission).[3]

All the various features of poetry indicate that the Psalms were written carefully and thoughtfully. They are compositions, the result of human effort to achieve effect. It has pleased God to use this form for the spiritual benefit and delight of those who are prepared to read and ponder. The more we understand the way poetry works, and the more we give ourselves to thoughtful, reflective, prayerful, meditative reading of the Psalms, so the more we will find them channels of spiritual insight and blessing.

Poetry in prophecy

We have already noticed that poetry is not confined to the Psalms. There are, of course, songs incorporated into the historical books. There are two songs of Moses, Exodus 15:1–18 and Deuteronomy 31:30–32:43. There is the song of Deborah and Barak, Judges 5. The very first human words recorded in the Bible are a brief love-song:

This is now bone of my bones
and flesh of my flesh;
she shall be called 'woman',
for she was taken out of man. (Genesis 2:23)

More importantly it needs to be noticed that a great deal of prophecy is written in the form of poetry. This means that generally speaking we do not look for a literal fulfilment of these particular prophecies. There are certainly some prophecies that have been fulfilled to the letter, but that does not mean we should expect such fulfilment in most cases. Consider Isaiah 54:11–12:

O afflicted city, lashed by storms and not comforted,
I will build you with stones of turquoise,
your foundations with sapphires.
I will make your battlements of rubies,
your gates of sparkling jewels,
and all your walls of precious stones.

Is this Jerusalem which is to be built? And is it to be built by the actual materials specified here? Is this actually referring to the rebuilding of a literal city at all? If not, what is this prophecy about? That is something to be decided by a close look at the context, and also, for its ultimate fulfilment, by throwing the light of the New Testament upon this passage.

Notes

1 *Collins English Dictionary* (London, Collins, 1985).
2 **George Lakoff** and **Mark Johnson,** *Metaphors We Live By* (Chicago, University of Chicago Press, 1980), p. 5; quoted in **D. Brent Sandy,** *Plowshares & Pruning Hooks* (Leicester, IVP, 2002), p. 74.
3 **Timothy Dudley-Smith,** *A House of Praise* (Oxford, Oxford University Press/Hope Publishing Company, 2003); p. 138; p. 142 for Psalm 34.

Narrative

Think of the way two different people recount what happened on their holidays. One rambles all over the place. Just when you are getting interested he says, 'Oh, I forgot ...' and then starts to go back to something else, breaking the flow of what he had been saying. The other, however, starts with the flight out, omits all the details that do not matter, highlights the interesting and humorous things that happened and rounds it all off with: 'And so we came back from the rain in Spain to be greeted by glorious sunshine at Heathrow!' The second person knows how to tell a story, the first, unfortunately, can be tedious and boring.

Psalm 23 is a poem, and poetry makes up about a third of the Bible. But the largest part of the Bible consists of narrative, about forty percent of the Old Testament and more than half of the New Testament. Behind written narrative lies story-telling, and it is likely that a great deal of the narrative portions of the Bible depend on stories about people and events that were passed on orally before these were woven into the continuous narrative of books like Genesis or Samuel and Kings. We are accustomed to think of these books as history and to emphasize that they are accurate in what they report. There is no doubt that this is important—God's Word is true in all that it says. The danger is, however, that we can miss two important features.

The first of these is the spiritual import and relevance of what the 'historical books' are telling us. The main books that we classify as historical in the Old Testament, Joshua to 2 Kings, come under the heading of 'The Former Prophets' in the Hebrew Bible. This reminds us that these books are not like secular history books, they are a divine commentary on Israel's history containing lessons for God's people. In particular they show that obedience brings blessing, while disobedience brings judgement and chastening. The books that we usually call the Prophets, Isaiah to Malachi, are known as 'The Latter Prophets' (except Daniel, which comes under 'The Writings', as also does Ruth).

The second feature is that the literary form of these books is narrative. That means that they are written to tell a story, and they include many episodes, or particular stories within the whole. If, for example, you consider the book of Genesis from chapter 12 on, you soon realize that it consists of the stories of Abraham, Jacob, and finally Joseph. And you can break down each of these into different episodes in their lives, more space being given to the more important events.

So how does a story work; what are the main elements that usually make up a story that holds your attention? We shall answer this by looking at one of the most well-known of Old Testament stories, that of David and Goliath (1 Samuel 17).

The first element is *setting*. The writer of 1 Samuel sets the scene for us in verses 1–3: 'Now the Philistines gathered their forces for war and assembled at Socoh in Judah. They pitched camp at Ephes Dammim, between Socoh and Azekah. Saul and the Israelites assembled and camped in the Valley of Elah and drew up their battle lines to meet the Philistines. The Philistines occupied one hill and the Israelites another, with the valley between them.' Although the names do not mean anything to us it is very easy to visualize the situation from this brief description. There are no unnecessary details. The Philistines have made an incursion into Judah and the two armies face each other with a valley between. As the story progresses it is not difficult to imagine David going down into the valley to meet Goliath, stopping as he does so to pick five stones from a stream flowing down.

Secondly there is *characterization*. The two main characters are obviously David and Goliath. David has already been described in the previous chapter (v. 11–12), so the spotlight is put on Goliath. Four verses describe this formidable giant of a man (v. 4–7). Everything we are told goes towards emphasizing his size and his strength. With his armour he appears invincible, with his weapons, deadly. It is not surprising that 'Saul and all the Israelites were dismayed and terrified'. What we are told about David is brief repetition of what we already know. He is the youngest of his family who tends his father's sheep (v. 14–15). He is a mere youth, still fresh-faced and good-looking. Moreover when he puts on the armour Saul provides for him he finds it strange and cumbersome, and has to take it off (v. 38–39). Just a few lines bring before us the frightening contrast between the threatening champion of the Philistines and the young David, who goes out to meet him in the name of God.

The third element is *plot*. Here the plot is a straightforward one. Israel is threatened by the Philistines. Saul and his army are challenged to provide a champion to fight against Goliath. If they send out a man and he is killed then the Israelites will become servants of the Philistines (v. 9). If they do send out someone on their behalf it looks certain that the giant will kill him; if they don't then surely the Philistines will enslave them anyway. How are they going to get out of this?

Many stories have plots similar to this. Here is a battle between good and evil. Evil looks sure to triumph, how can the weak and the good overcome the power that evil has on its side? Thousands of detective stories, thrillers and war stories have exactly the same basic plot, and it is the ingenuity and artistry of writers that keeps people reading the same basic story in all its varied forms. If you think of the Bible itself, so many of the stories are like this. It starts with the devil and Adam and Eve, and in a real way the unfolding story of the Bible is the story of the struggle between the offspring of the serpent and the offspring of the woman (Genesis 3:15). And so we have Jacob and Esau, Joseph and his brothers, Moses and Pharaoh, Samuel and Saul, Elijah and Ahab with his wife Jezebel, Esther and Haman, Jesus and the scribes, Pharisees and chief priests.

Of course the plot in 1 Samuel 17 is a very simple one yet it is this that awakens our interest and holds our attention. We want to know how the story is going to end. We want to know whether the problem facing Israel is going to be resolved and how that takes place. Many other stories have a far more complicated plot and it is the resolution of the plot, and the twists and turns on the way to the resolution that makes for a good story. If we think of the story-line of the Bible as a whole then we see a much more complicated plot with the backslidings of Israel and times when it seems as if God has forgotten his promises and is no longer answering prayer. But with the coming of Christ and his crucifixion and resurrection we are in a position to see that the decisive victory has been achieved, even though the story has not yet ended and we have to live through our own time and place in it.

In many stories the plot ultimately revolves around two characters, the antagonist—the enemy, the one who is evil—and the protagonist, the hero, the champion of good. That, of course, is exactly what we have here. The

Philistines, the Israelites, Saul, David's brothers, are all involved, but ultimately it all comes down to who is going to win, David or Goliath?

A further element is *suspense*. If a writer can hold back the decisive resolution this creates suspense: the reader wants to know what is going to happen and his interest and desire is stimulated by having to wait. Writers use various devices to create suspense. Dickens does so by introducing other characters whose lives and actions impinge on the main characters, but who at the same time delay the ending that the reader is anticipating and hoping for—perhaps the marriage of the leading characters, once the antagonist or antagonists have met their fate, whatever it may be. In doing this he brings in many sub-plots, which in turn have an interest of their own.

The writer of 1 Samuel introduces suspense by telling his story slowly and bringing in a great deal of detail as he builds towards the climax of verses 48–51. In verses 12–15 he takes our attention back to Bethlehem and Jesse's family before returning to the battlefield for one verse (v. 16). As the story develops we are reminded again of the threat overhanging Israel (v. 23–24). Before David goes out against Goliath the scorn of his older brothers has to be overcome (v. 28–31), his dismissal by Saul (v. 33), and the unsuitability of the armour Saul provided (v. 38–39). David is greeted by the rage of Goliath (v. 42–44). After David's response of faith and assurance, (v. 45–47), the story moves quickly to David's amazing victory.

Another example of suspense can be seen in the book of Esther. Chapter 3 tells of the threat of Haman against the Jews throughout the whole Persian empire, see especially verses 12–15. In chapter 4 Mordecai enlists the help of Queen Esther, and the first verse of chapter 5 sees her appearing before the king. By the end of that chapter the situation appears to be even worse with a gallows being built on which to hang Mordecai. Chapter 6 begins with a sleepless night spent by the king, and it isn't until chapter 7 that Esther actually brings her request to the king, and chapter 8 ends with the rejoicing of the Jews over the defeat of their enemies.

The final element is *resolution*; the problem is solved, the difficulty is overcome, there is a just and satisfactory outcome in the end. 'So David triumphed over the Philistine with a sling and a stone; without a sword in his hand he struck down the Philistine and killed him. David ran and stood over him. He took hold of the Philistine's sword and drew it from his scabbard. After he killed him, he cut off his head with the sword. When the Philistines saw that their hero was dead, they turned and ran. Then the men of Israel and Judah surged forward with a shout and pursued the Philistines to the entrance of Gath and to the gates of Ekron' (v. 50–52).

It is important not to misunderstand what is being said here. It is not being argued that the writer of 1 Samuel consciously set out to give attention to these five elements, though we need not assume that there was no conventional way of writing at that time. The point is that when you analyse a good story you generally find that these are the features that are well written and make the story what it is. Nor are we talking about the difference between fact and fiction. Your holidays are not fiction; but they can be recounted well and interestingly or otherwise. The writer of the story of David and Goliath is dealing with fact but he writes it in a powerful and gripping way. And so it is with much of the Bible, both in the Old Testament and the New.

Does it help us if we have some understanding of how narrative—story—works? I think it does. It helps to give us the right mind-set as we approach a particular passage. If we have been put off history, perhaps at school, by a history text-book; or if we have simply bought into the view that history is boring, then when we are told that certain books of the Bible are history we will have the wrong attitude of mind towards them right at the start. If we read them simply looking for a moral here or there, or just to pick out a verse which seems to speak to us, we are again approaching them in the wrong way. But if we expect them to be absorbing, interesting—if we have some idea of how they work—we shall read with anticipation and surrender ourselves to the flow of the narrative.

When you read the stories in the Bible there are two steps you need to take. Firstly, read with imagination. Let the text enable you to envisage the scene and see the drama unfolding before your eyes. I do not mean, imagine all sorts of details that are not to be found in the text, but use your imagination to see what is there. After all, it doesn't take much imagination to see two camps on hills opposite each other with a valley between. Nor to see a stream with stones worn smooth lying on its bed, nor to see the contrast between Goliath with his size, his armour and weapons, and

David, so young, so unprotected and with such an apparently inadequate weapon. Many Christians have been suspicious of imagination, partly because they have come across examples of its abuse when people read things into the Bible. This is a great pity. The ability to imagine is a great gift from God and enables us to enter into the world of the Bible, and the events of which it speaks. Warren Wiersbe, in his excellent book, *Preaching and Teaching with Imagination,*[1] has collected a number of quotations about imagination. Here are two: 'The great instrument of moral good is the imagination' (Percy Bysshe Shelley). 'Imagination is the eye of the soul' (Joseph Joubert).

However there is a further step. Stories in the Bible are to be read not only with imagination but also with involvement. Reading with involvement enables us to put ourselves into the story, both as spectators, but also identifying ourselves with the main characters. Some people have a gift in this respect, and find it easy to see themselves in Bible narratives. Nearly all of us can identify with David in 1 Samuel 17. Not that most of us are likely to feel that we would have had the faith and courage that he displayed. Nevertheless we can see how sure he was of God's protection. We can feel how vulnerable he was, how dependent on his stone being slung with deadly accuracy. Generally speaking it is with the hero in the story that we are likely to identify.

But it is not difficult to enter into Goliath's feelings as he found himself confronted with David. We have all met brash youngsters ourselves! The fact is that we can see ourselves in Scribes and Pharisees, in Pharaoh, in Ahab and Jezebel, and any other bad character to be found in the Bible. The same sins that blossomed in their lives are found at least in seed form in our hearts. Stories well told draw us into the narrative. But we must let the actual text fashion and guide our involvement.

What, then, is the value of narrative? In the first place narrative is a form that awakens interest and holds our attention, it makes you want to read on and find out what happened next. The novelist E.M. Forster said of narrative that it 'can only have one merit: that of making the audience want to know what happens next. And conversely it can only have one fault: that of making the audience not want to know what happens next'.[2] You don't want to put a good book down! Perhaps one practical point is important here. When reading the Bible, and especially the narrative portions, don't simply read ten verses, or even one chapter. Read to the end of the story, or the end of the episode. To divide up 1 Samuel 17 into three or four days reading would be to miss the whole thrust and sense of the whole.

Secondly, narrative presents truth in practical situations. Here we see life as it was and as it is. The more doctrinal parts of the Bible are illustrated in the narratives, both on a large scale with the nation of Israel, and at the personal level. Here we have temptation and sin, obedience and disobedience, godliness and ungodliness, the difficulties, trials and struggles of sinful humans called by God's grace to be his people, exhibited before us. We see the complexities of life, the decisions that have to be made, the ebb and flow of faith even in the godliest of people. Living with them in the pages of Scripture enables us more adequately to live as we ought to live in our generation and circumstances.

Finally, the narrative passages of the Bible demonstrate that in the last analysis God himself is the great protagonist and hero, as indeed he is in 1 Samuel 17: 'the whole world will know that there is a God in Israel' (v.46). God himself is creator, provider, saviour, guide, restorer and final reward. All history is his story. The Bible has one great over-arching story line from creation through fall and redemption to the final consummation. It is the story of the triune God and his grace.

Notes

1 **Warren Weirsbe,** *Preaching and Teaching with Imagination* (Grand Rapids, Baker Book House, 1997.).

2 Quoted by **Leland Ryken,** *Words of Delight, A Literary Introduction to the Bible* (Grand Rapids, Baker, 1987), p. 63. The quotation comes from **E.M. Forster,** *Aspects of the Novel* (Harmondsworth, Penguin, 1974), p. 35.

Two more literary features

There are two other features which occur both in poetry and narrative in the Bible. These are to be found in both Testaments.

Chiasm

The first of these is called chiasm (or chiasmus). This takes its name from the Greek letter *chi* which is written like an English letter X. In the poetic form this is because there is a cross over between the two lines of the couplet:

'I will destroy the wisdom of the wise;

the intelligence of the intelligent I will frustrate.' (1 Corinthians 1:19)

In this case the verb comes at the beginning of the first line, but at the end of the second line. This makes you stop and think and gives a certain emphasis to the verse. It makes it more memorable and tends to stress the verbs because they come first and last.

Chiasm is not restricted to poetry. William Hendriksen draws attention to its use in Colossians 1:16: 'Note the criss-cross or chiastic manner in which this thought is expressed:

'For in him were created all things
in the heavens and on the earth

the visible and the invisible.'

Here clearly the visible creatures are those viewed as on earth: the invisible as in heaven.'[1]

Chiasm can also be used in an extended way. Look at Deuteronomy chapter 8. We can express its structure in this way:

A[1] Follow the Lord who swore an oath to your forefathers (v. 1).

B^1 Remember the Lord who led you through the wilderness (v. 2–6).

C^1 Describes the good land (v. 7–10a) ending 'When you have eaten and are full.'

D Praise God and do not forget him (v. 10b,11).

C^2 Describes the good land (v. 12–13) beginning 'When you have eaten and are full.'

B^2 Do not forget the Lord who brought you through the wilderness (v. 14–17).

A^2 Remember the Lord who swore an oath to your forefathers (v. 18).

So verses 12–18 are a mirror image of the opening verses, 1–10a. When you see this you realize that the key verses are 10b–11. This is the heart of the passage and the main message of this chapter. Clearly a more complicated chiasm like this indicates careful thought on the part of its author. He uses it to stress what is important in the passage. It is not always easy to recognize such chiasms, but careful consideration of a passage may reveal it. Recognition is easier in the original languages, especially in poetry, as chiasm is not generally used in English and most translations would use a more English idiom.

Irony

Irony picks out incongruities. There is often a grim humour associated with it, and a dramatic irony in the way a biblical narrative is presented. An example of this occurs towards the close of Matthew 26. From verse 57–68 we are shown Jesus in the high priest's house before the Sanhedrin bearing a faithful witness while false witnesses are brought against him. In the next passage we are shown Peter outside in the courtyard denying with oaths that he knows Jesus. The contrast is appalling. There is a tragic irony here. A briefer, but almost as pointed, example occurs in Jonah chapter 1. In the great storm the pagan sailors call upon their gods, while Jonah, the prophet of the Lord, is asleep below decks (verses 4–6).

A somewhat different example comes again in Matthew in the last two chapters. At the end of chapter 27 the chief priests and Pharisees go to Pilate so that a guard can be set over the tomb of Jesus in case his disciples come and steal his body and say he has been raised from the dead. In chapter 28:11–15, after the resurrection, the same people go to the soldiers that make up the guard and bribe them to say that the disciples came and stole the body of Jesus! Of course the irony in a biblical narrative is never a mere literary device. It is used to portray dramatically the irony that exists in the situation being described.

Note

1 **William Hendrikesen,** *Colossians and Philemon* (Grand Rapids, Baker Book House, 1964), p. 73.

Prophecy

M any Bible readers find the prophetic books among the most difficult to understand. And there are prophetic portions in other books, for example Matthew 24 and its parallels in Mark and Luke. We have already noticed that much prophecy is given in the form of poetry. What else do we need to know when approaching prophetic parts of the Bible?

Prophets proclaim God's Word

Consider Moses. In Exodus 6:28–29 we read: 'Now when the LORD spoke to Moses in Egypt, he said to him, "I am the LORD. Tell Pharaoh king of Egypt everything I tell you."' This is the essence of prophetic ministry. The prophet speaks everything that God tells him. This is underlined by what we read next in Exodus. Moses objects that as he speaks with faltering lips Pharaoh is not likely to listen to him. The Lord replies: 'See, I have made you like God to Pharaoh, and your brother Aaron will be your prophet. You are to say everything I command you, and your brother Aaron is to tell Pharaoh to let the Israelites go out of his country' (7:1–2). Not only does this show us God's kindness in providing Moses' brother to support him, but it also illustrates clearly the nature of prophecy. Moses will be like God and Aaron will be his spokesman, his prophet.

Moses is actually the best example of a prophet because God spoke to him 'mouth to mouth' (Numbers 12:8, literal translation) and he is the prototype of the true and final prophet whom God will yet send into the world to reveal his will. 'I will raise up for them a prophet like you from among their brothers; I will put my words in his mouth, and he will tell them everything I command him' (Deuteronomy 18:18). This was fulfilled, as Peter indicates, in the coming and ministry of Jesus Christ (Acts 3:22–23).

It must be understood that though the prophets spoke God's Word this does not mean that they were simply secretaries speaking what was dictated to them. Rather, God put *his* Word into *their* mouths. They spoke in their own language, out of their own upbringing and cultural background. What they spoke was authentically their word, as well as truly his.

It is in the context of prophets speaking the Word of God that foretelling comes. God used the prophets both to warn of coming judgement and also to give promises of future blessing. In this way foretelling is integral to prophecy, but it is not the essence of prophecy. There are two points that need to be borne in mind. First, most of the foretelling was about events that would take place in the immediate future. For example, Jeremiah 6:1 says:

'Flee for safety, people of Benjamin!
  Flee from Jerusalem!
Sound the trumpet in Tekoa!
  Raise the signal over Beth Hakkerem!
For disaster looms out of the north,
  even terrible destruction.

From our point of view the fulfilment of those words took place centuries ago when the Babylonians came and devastated Judah, captured Jerusalem and took many of the people away into exile. Second, sometimes the prophesied future is conditional. The most obvious example comes in the book of Jonah. Jonah's message was, 'Forty more days and Nineveh will be overturned.' But as a result of the repentance of the whole city from the king down, 'God saw what they did and how they turned from their evil ways, he had compassion and did not bring upon them the destruction he had threatened' (Jonah 3:4,10).

The prophets spoke to the people of their own day

In understanding prophecy the starting point has to be what the prophets were saying to the people to whom they prophesied. They had a message from God which they were delivering to actual people in a certain situation. There are many oracles of rebuke because of sin, which often include judgement, either threatened or implied. In many cases these are at least implied calls to repentance. By 'oracle' is meant a prophetic word, a prophetic message addressed to a particular people, a unit of prophecy (see

Isaiah 13–23). Complementary to these are oracles of deliverance and salvation. It is usually not difficult to see how oracles like this can be applied to today's readers.

For example, in Isaiah 1:10ff, God speaks to Judah in these terms:

Hear the word of the LORD,
    you rulers of Sodom;
listen to the law of our God,
    you people of Gomorrah!
'The multitude of your sacrifices—
    what are they to me?' says the LORD.
I have more than enough of burnt offerings,
    of rams and the fat of fattened animals;
I have no pleasure
    in the blood of bulls and lambs and goats.

Here it is clear enough that the rulers and people of Judah have degenerated until they can be compared to the people of Sodom and Gomorrah. The particular fault which is highlighted is that of simply multiplying sacrifices. There are at least two implications. The first is that the people seem to think that the answer to their sins is to bring many sacrifices rather than to turn from those sins in repentance. The second is their assumption that God must be pleased with the mere offering of sacrifices apart from the attitude of heart in which they are offered. The applications to be drawn are obvious. Notice also the irony here. God had instituted the sacrificial system, yet he has no pleasure in the use Judah made of it!

Follow the New Testament lead in interpreting Old Testament prophecy

In general the New Testament takes what the Old Testament prophets said to Israel or Judah and applies this to the people of God in the present era. For example, in Romans 10 Paul applies to faith in Jesus Christ Isaiah 28:16, 'Anyone who trusts in him will never be put to shame', and Joel 2:32, 'Everyone who calls on the name of the Lord will be saved.' He also deduces from the language that this applies as much to Gentiles as to Jews—

'*Everyone* who calls.' This is actually very similar to the example we have just considered from Isaiah 1. Paul is bringing out the spiritual principle of trusting God enshrined in the Old Testament and applying it to the present age, focusing more directly on Jesus himself.

But the New Testament goes beyond this. It applies Isaiah 53 with its picture of the suffering servant of the LORD directly to Jesus (Matthew 8:17; Acts 8:32–35; 1 Peter 2:22–25; following the lead of Jesus himself, Matthew 20:28). So some of the things that the prophets wrote about look beyond their own age and are fulfilled in the messianic age, that is the age inaugurated by the coming of the Christ. This is particularly true of the oracles of salvation.

We have in our house a picture of the Alhambra in Granada, Spain, painted by my wife. One of the features of the Alhambra that enhances its beauty is that it is set against the backdrop of the snowy peaks of the Sierra Nevada. So as you look at the picture, the Alhambra itself—a Moorish palace—occupies centre stage. Behind it are two lines of mountains, then the snows behind them next to the bright blue of a southern Mediterranean sky. It makes one picture, but if you travel from Granada to the Sierra you realize that there are miles between the mountain ranges.

Prophecy can be like that. It may look as if one event is being foretold, but in fact there may be a long 'distance' between one part of the prophecy and the next. For example, Isaiah 9:6–7 says:

For to us a child is born,
  to us a son is given ...
He will reign on David's throne
  and over his kingdom.

The fulfilment of the first two lines refers, of course, to the birth of Jesus Christ. When, however, did he begin to reign on David's throne? We might argue that in a sense it began with the commencement of his ministry. Or, more likely, we would say after his resurrection, all authority in heaven and earth being given to him. Yet, it could be argued that the final form of his reign awaits his second coming. Similarly, Malachi 3 begins like this: 'See, I will send my messenger, who will prepare the way before me. Then suddenly the Lord you are seeking will come to his temple … But who can endure the day of his coming? Who can stand when he appears?' The opening words also obviously identify this coming of the Lord with the ministry of Jesus Christ, for it was John the Baptist who was the messenger who prepared the way. But it seems very likely as if the next verse looks on to his second coming.

Amazingly the same prophecy can have several fulfilments. If you read Isaiah 43:14–21 you will see that it pictures God's deliverance of his people from Babylon in terms that are reminiscent of the Exodus deliverance. But does the deliverance from Babylon exhaust this prophecy (and others like it: Isaiah 35:6–8; 42:16; 48:17–21; 55:12)? In Luke's Gospel Jesus' death is spoken of as his 'exodus' (9:31), and the idea of the Exodus deliverance seems to be recalled (for example, see Colossians 1:13). Passages like Isaiah 43:14–21 can also find their fulfilment in the deliverance from sin which those who believe in Jesus Christ experience. In the final analysis they find their fulfilment in a return, not to Jerusalem, but to God himself and the heavenly city and its glory.

Apocalyptic

This is a specialized form of prophecy which takes its name from the Greek word that means 'revelation' or 'unveiling'. The name of the last book in the Bible, Revelation, is sometimes transliterated from Greek into English as 'The Apocalypse'. In verse one of that book it is called a 'revelation' and in verse three it is described as 'prophecy'. A great deal of the difficulty in understanding the book of Revelation arises from its form as apocalyptic. Apocalyptic is also found in the Old Testament, particularly in Daniel (see, for example, chapters 7–8), but also in Isaiah, Ezekiel, Joel and Zechariah. In the New Testament it is also found in our Lord's discourse in Matthew 24 (cf. Mark 13; Luke 21), in 1 and 2 Thessalonians and 2 Peter. In the period between the end of the Old Testament and the coming of John the Baptist there was a great deal of apocalyptic literature produced among the Jews. It is not possible to make an absolutely clear-cut distinction between ordinary prophecy and apocalyptic, but the main features of the latter can be described.

One of the most obvious of these is that the imagery becomes much more difficult, and can often seem bizarre. There is an important distinction here. Psalm 23 gives clear imagery which can easily be visualized in our minds. Apocalyptic is quite different. It uses images which are impossible to put together and hold together. For example, in Revelation 9 we have locusts that are like horses that have tails like scorpions, faces like humans, hair like women and teeth like lions. It is impossible to visualize creatures like this, and it is important not to try to do so. We are not intended to imagine what these apparently composite creatures look like. Rather each descriptive phrase tells us something new about these creatures—which are not literal locusts in any case, but are as destructive and harmful as locusts. While prophecy makes use of imagery and metaphor, apocalyptic gives visions that are mysterious and strange, going far beyond anything we see or know in this world.

A second feature of apocalyptic is that it is directed at different people, and has a different purpose, from most other prophecy. By and large prophecy is directed to a mixed people and calls them to repentance and a new obedience to the Lord. Old Testament prophecy addresses Israel (or Judah) as God's people, frequently as disobedient and in danger of judgement. Apocalyptic addresses those who are true to God, the faithful remnant, and its purpose is to comfort and strengthen them in spite of the suffering and opposition they are experiencing. It assures them that behind what appears to be happening in this world God is working his purpose out and will yet vindicate himself and deliver them.

This leads to the third main feature. Apocalyptic is about what God is going to do. It is not a call to his people to remember their responsibilities. It comes in the context of abounding evil to which the only answer is the intervention of God himself. For this reason it ultimately points to the final end of all things; the final judgement of all men and women; the just punishment of the unrighteous (including all the powers of darkness); and the final glory of God in which all the faithful share for ever.

If we return for a moment to Revelation 9 we can begin to see how we can make some sense of apocalyptic visions. There are two visions here (note 'I saw', v.1 and 17). The overwhelming impression is of strange creatures that are horrible, terrible and hurtful. That is the impression we are supposed to gain. The first vision is of locusts. In the Old Testament swarms of locusts often appear as judgements of God (e.g. Joel 1:1–2:11). (The book of Revelation is full of allusions to the Old Testament and many of its themes are rooted there. These need to be traced out in interpreting its visions, but it is not possible here to do more than refer to that in passing.) So the locusts represent judgements from God. This is confirmed further by noticing that it is a star from heaven that is given the key to the abyss to open it and release the locusts (v. 1–2). Similarly, in the second vision the four angels have 'been kept ready for this very hour and day and month and year'. Heaven is in control here. A further point is that these judgements are only for 'those people who did not have the seal of God on their foreheads' (v. 4). They are judgements for the impenitent, who will not repent even when they suffer greatly (v. 20–21). The locusts come out of the abyss, so they represent the forces of evil, the powers of darkness. Evil, sin, can appear attractive to people, but it is actually harmful, hurtful, bringing all sorts of bondage and misery in its train.

Perhaps this is sufficient as the briefest introduction to a chapter like this. What are the lessons for God's people? There are several. Don't envy unbelievers who perhaps appear to enjoy life even though they trample on God's commandments. God will judge them, and in the end his judgements will be severe indeed. Remember, every Christian has been sealed by God; he knows those who are his, and distinguishes them from others. Keep faithful to him, even though there is violence and suffering in the world and it seems as if all hell has been let loose—up to a point it has and may yet be more fully let loose!

Literality

J esus said to Nicodemus, 'I tell you the truth, no-one can see the kingdom of God unless he is born again.' Nicodemus replied, 'How can a man be born when he is old? Surely he cannot enter a second time into his mother's womb and be born?' Nicodemus's mistake was to take the words of our Lord literally. We take up again a point which was touched on when considering metaphor.

Evangelicals have always tended to lay an emphasis on interpreting the Bible literally. Over against the fanciful interpretations that had become customary in the Roman Catholic Church of the time, the Reformers said that the literal sense of the words is the proper sense. More recently over against the tendency of liberals to explain away miracles, or to introduce the categories of myth and legend into the Bible, evangelicals have again emphasized the literal truth of the Bible. But those who have studied the Bible carefully have always known that the situation is a complex one.

First of all, what the Reformers were concerned to establish is that understanding must be based on the natural sense of the words. In the example of our Lord's words to Nicodemus the question is, what is the natural sense of Jesus' words? It is very possible for someone who usually thinks in physical, material, human terms to understand Jesus as Nicodemus did. The Jews of his day thought of the kingdom of God in materialistic terms. They looked for the overthrow of the Romans, with independence and prosperity in their land. For most of us as Christians it is perfectly natural for us to think of Jesus speaking about a spiritual birth. Of course, this is partly because we know what Jesus went on to say to Nicodemus. It has become natural for us to understand 'born again' as a metaphor for the radical, spiritual change effected by the Holy Spirit which makes a person spiritually alive, bringing him or her into God's kingdom, so enabling spiritual understanding.

When we stop to think about it, the situation may be a little complicated in the case of Nicodemus, but the principle is a sound one—follow the natural sense of the words. The Reformers knew perfectly well that there is poetry in the Bible and metaphor, parable and other genres. They knew also that in many ways the Old Testament prepares for and points forward to Jesus Christ. Nevertheless, they were very concerned to nip in the bud all fanciful and forced interpretations of the Word of God. The Reformers had seen the harm this can do, and the way it shuts the Bible up from the ordinary reader. So, read poetry as poetry, understand metaphor as metaphor, but follow the natural sense of the words and sentences.

Secondly, evangelicals are concerned to accept the historical truth of what is written as straightforward truth in the Bible. This is often what is meant by saying we must understand the Bible literally. Of course, parables are not to be understood as literally true. It may also be the case that stories of true events may function in the way myth functions. If myth is defined as 'sacred stories set in a time different from the narrator(s), expressing an understanding of reality that justifies some of the institutions of the society …' then such stories are to be found in the Bible. It is highly misleading to call them myths, however, as generally myths are understood to be fictional. What is written as sober history is to be accepted as such, even if it includes miracles, for the Creator is able to intervene in his own creation.

Thirdly, evangelicals often speak about believing the Bible to be literally true when they are thinking about the teaching of the Bible. We believe in propositional truth. That is to say, when the Bible says, 'God is love', or 'the Word became flesh', or 'all have sinned and fall short of the glory of God', or 'the gift of God is eternal life in Christ Jesus our Lord', we accept those as statements of truth.

Note

1 **J.W. Rogerson,** 'Myth' in **R.J. Coggins** and **J.L. Houlden** (eds), *Dictionary of Biblical Interpretation* (London, SCM, 1960) p. 481.

Words and sentences

The building blocks of writing are words, but words have no meaning unless they are in sentences. Some sentences have only one word— 'Fire!' 'Help!' for example—but in that case they need a context if we are to understand exactly what they mean. Either a context in life, or else a context of other sentences to show what the one-word sentence means. The sentence is the basic unit of meaning, though of course sentences can be very long and involved. At the same time, a sentence has to be read in the context of the paragraph in which it occurs. Jesus' words, 'Here are my mother and my brothers' (Matthew 12:49), do not mean what they appear to mean if they are taken out of their context. He was, in fact, pointing to his disciples and went on to say, 'For whoever does the will of my Father in heaven is my brother and sister and mother (v. 50)'. Context is always important, both the immediate context and the wider context, including the book in which the sentence occurs and the place of the book in the whole of the Bible.

The meaning of words

Many words have a range of meaning. As we have seen, poetry often exploits this, and narrative can do the same. But words generally take a precise meaning from the sentence they are in. For example, the word 'image' is used in various ways in the Bible but in Daniel 3:1 it simply refers to a large statue made out of gold (or at least covered in gold). The word 'flesh' is also used in several different ways, but in John 1:14, 'The Word became flesh', it refers to the Word taking a human nature especially emphasizing the bodily aspect of this. In Hebrews 12:2 we read of Jesus, 'who for the joy set before him endured the cross'. The word translated 'for' is a word which frequently means 'instead of' and some have argued that it ought to have that meaning here. However, it also has the meaning 'for the sake of', and the context indicates that this is the proper meaning in this place.

Words often have shades of meaning and can be used in ways which only those who are familiar with the language recognize. In English 'talk' and 'speak' are very similar and can often be used interchangeably. Yet they are not precisely the same. We might say, 'He talked and talked all evening', but we would not say, 'He spoke and spoke all evening'. The difference is seen even more clearly if we think of the nouns. A speech is not the same as a talk. We even use different verbs with the nouns, 'she made a speech', but 'she gave a talk'. It would be very difficult to convey such nuances in translation. This book assumes its readers will read the Bible in translation, but it is important to realize that there are nuances and shades of meaning in Hebrew and Greek that are almost impossible to put into English. It is for this reason that for close study a good commentary is necessary. Just knowing what the Greek or Hebrew word is or the possible meanings a dictionary gives is not sufficient to appreciate what a word means in a particular place.

This is one of the reasons why translation is so difficult. In order to translate as accurately as possible translators have to know the original language thoroughly and be at home in the culture so that they can pick up nuances of meaning. Then they must also be able to express those nuances in the idiom of the receptor language; that is, the language they are translating into. In some cases this may be almost impossible to do—though the meaning can be explained in a commentary. We need to be very thankful for the work of translators, but recognize that for close study it can be valuable to compare several translations and also use commentaries.

Present usage not past meaning

In the past some Bible scholars tended to pay too much attention to the etymology—or original meaning—of words. But words often change their meaning over time. In 1 Thessalonians 4:15 the Authorized Version reads, 'we which are alive and remain unto the coming of the Lord shall not prevent them which are asleep'. Here we have the original meaning of the word 'prevent', which is 'come before' from the Latin. Now, however, the word means 'keep from happening', and no modern translation would use 'prevent'. The word 'nice' once meant 'ignorant' (again from Latin), and the word 'fabulous' meant 'legendary' or 'imaginary'. Such words have lost their original meanings and it is no help in understanding present meaning to go back to what they once meant (though you can often see how the meaning developed and changed).

Sometimes the supposed etymological meaning is very doubtful. For example, it is not uncommon to hear it said that the Greek word for 'church', *ekklesia,* literally means 'the called out ones'. This is because the word is constructed from *ek,* 'out of', and *kaleo,* to call. But there is no evidence at all of the use of a verb *ekkaleo* in the New Testament and it is widely agreed that the word simply means 'assembly' or 'congregation'. Another example of the same thing is the word translated 'only begotten' in some versions. But the original Greek word is related to the verb 'to be, become' rather than the verb 'to beget'. This means that the New International Version's 'one and only' is correct. The idea of 'begotten' is, of course, implicit in the word 'Son', so there is no theological implication in the change. The point is that it is contemporary usage, and usage in context, which give words their meaning.

Denotation and connotation

These words are used to describe an important distinction. What a word *denotes* is what it actually refers to. The word 'shadow' refers to the patch of darkness thrown on to the ground by some object which prevents the sun from shining directly there. A shadow in a valley suggests one side of the valley which is dark and gloomy because the hillside throws its shadow over that part. But 'shadow' can also *connote* a dark and sad experience: 'The accident to Mrs Smith cast a shadow over the whole family.' Similarly Christians sometimes talk about a 'valley' experience, or at the opposite end of the scale a 'mountain top' experience, because both of these words have connotations for them.

A word may have a number of different connotations, but in a specific context only one of those is appropriate. The word 'rod' in Psalm 23 denotes a piece of wood or stick. In our culture the word 'rod' would most probably mean a fishing rod, but this is obviously not the case in the psalm. It is sometimes used in the Old Testament as a metaphor for discipline, the rod of correction, or to indicate authority when it is translated as 'sceptre'. Most likely here it refers to a heavy stick or cudgel which would be used for the protection of the sheep, in this way distinguishing it from the shepherd's 'staff'. David used some weapon in protecting his sheep from wild animals (note the word 'struck' in 1 Samuel 17:35). So 'rod' connotes protection, defence. In the dark valley where enemies may lurk, David draws comfort from knowing that the Lord is his protector and has the appropriate weapons that are needed.

Association and evocation

Here are two more words which can enlarge our understanding of the way words are used. 'Associations' have looser connections with a word than connotations. Many words can spark off a train of thought, because of the associations that the word has in the mind of the reader. *He leads me beside quiet waters*. Particularly when you think of the hot, dry Middle East, 'waters' suggests refreshment, coolness, thirst satisfied. Trees grow beside waters, so there is shade as well. Here is an oasis in a dry and thirsty land.

Evocation refers to what words or sentences evoke, or call out. This is similar to association but not exactly the same. The words themselves evoke a mood, a feeling, even without a person realizing quite what is happening or the way in which the words work. *He makes me lie down in green pastures, he leads me beside quiet waters* evokes a sense of peace, tranquillity, rest, satisfaction, safety, calm, sufficiency. Without knowing precisely how we should understand *green pastures* or *quiet waters* we feel a sense of calm and rest called out by the picture itself.

Words reveal

I have a letter written by my mother about a fortnight before she died. She was at that time confined to bed and in constant pain. What she had to say in the letter is now irrelevant. But the thing that struck me on reading it years later was how alive she seems. I received a forceful impression of vibrancy, alertness and vitality. Of course she wasn't intending to convey such an impression, but somehow that is what comes across.

The biblical writers often reveal a lot about themselves; their concerns, priorities, feelings and desires. David became king and won great battles. Even before he was crowned he was lauded to the skies by the women of Israel: 'Saul has slain his thousands, and David his tens of thousands.' Yet he thinks of himself as a sheep, when he thinks of his relationship to God. Humility shines out of Psalm 23.

Some writers reveal their feelings more explicitly than others, Jeremiah for example. In the New Testament Paul particularly opens up his heart in 2 Corinthians. In his first letter to the church at Corinth he deals more objectively with the problems and questions in the church. In his second letter his personal relationship with the church is much more prominent: 'I wrote to you out of great distress and anguish of heart and with many tears, not to grieve you but to let you know the depth of my love for you' (2:4).

Even when a writer does not express his feelings so explicitly, it is often possible to pick up his concerns and gain indications of his character. This may be the case even when we don't know who he is. The writer to the Hebrews keeps himself very much in the background throughout most of his letter. Right at the end you read, 'Brothers, I urge you to bear with my word of exhortation' (13:22). This indicates his concern for the Hebrews, and his hope that they would receive and submit to what he has written. But a few verses earlier he said this, 'I particularly urge you to pray so that I may be restored to you soon' (v. 19). Suddenly you have a remarkable insight into the character of this man. He has had to speak very severely in places in his letter. His warnings have been urgent and serious. The situation is one where apostasy is threatening. But he is not content simply to send off a letter from afar. Here is someone who obviously has ministered among them previously and who asks for prayer that he may soon be back in the thick of the fray, warning, pleading, encouraging, bringing them back to fix their eyes on Jesus.

So as you read, keep your eyes open for ways in which the writers of the books of the Bible reveal themselves. Real people, men of God to be sure, but also people with real feelings, wrote the Bible. There is much to be gained from learning about them.

The power of words

The word 'rhetoric' is not much in favour these days. 'Empty rhetoric!' we might say about something that a politician has said. It is often thought that Paul also resisted the use of current Greek rhetoric, 'My message and my preaching were not with wise and persuasive words, but with a demonstration of the Spirit's power' (1 Corinthians 2:4). But if Paul repudiated the tricks of the orator's trade and what we now call 'spin', as he did, that does not mean that he did not speak, and write, with great power. There is what we might call the rhetoric of conviction and emotion, and this is to be found again and again in his letters. You can tell that his heart and soul are engaged in what he wrote. His words come out of a heart inflamed by the Holy Spirit. So when he contrasts 'wise and persuasive words' with 'a demonstration of the Spirit's power' he is not meaning that he preached in a cold, undemonstrative manner in flat, unimaginative language. He means that there was nothing false, nothing artificial, nothing merely worked up about the way in which he spoke. Just as people felt the power of what he said, so we are to recognize the power with which he writes. And not just Paul, but all the biblical writers, in their different ways. One of the problems with some commentaries is that they treat language which comes from the depths of spiritual concern and desire in a detached, scientific type of way. If a commentary does not help us to feel the pulse of the writer then to that extent it has failed.

Words do things

There is a tendency for many of us to think that words simply inform. Of course words do inform, but they are used to do much more than that. Think of a court of law. A prosecuting counsel uses words to convict a person. A jury can pronounce a person not guilty. A judge can sentence someone to life imprisonment, and he can stipulate the minimum number of years that should mean. Passages in the Bible are like this. God, through the human writer, may bring a case against a person or nation. So Micah says to Israel,

Hear, O mountains, the LORD's accusation,
    listen, you everlasting foundations of the earth.
For the LORD has a case against his people;
    he is lodging a charge against Israel. (6:2)

And God may act as a judge:

The LORD takes his place in court;
    he rises to judge the people.

The LORD enters into judgement
   against the elders and leaders of the people (Isaiah 3:13–14).

In the Bible we come across promises, warnings, exhortations, encouragements. These are intended to bring about certain effects in readers. Promises produce hope; warnings encourage caution; exhortations stir and stimulate; encouragements comfort and strengthen. The Bible not only teaches, it rebukes and corrects (2 Timothy 3:16). Peter stimulates his readers to wholesome thinking (2 Peter 3:1). Words can make you laugh or cry; they can make you angry, or sympathetic, glad, thoughtful or enthusiastic. Unless the words of the Bible produce the effects in you that are appropriate to what they are saying you have not understood them properly or appreciated them as you should. Words do things. In particular, God acts by his words. Ask yourself what effects Psalm 23 and other passages should have on you. Read, allowing the passage to make its own impression upon your consciousness.

Words call for a response

This is one stage further. Words do make their own effect upon those who read them, but they also call for a response. This is certainly true of the Bible. Just as the prophets and apostles called for a response to their oral preaching, so their written words call for the same. Of course, the response varies depending on who the reader is and what his or her condition is. Much of the Bible intends to effect changes in knowledge, understanding, outlook and behaviour. But that leads us on to the next part of the book, the world of the reader, the world in front of the text.

Review and further study

1. One of the most important questions to ask before reading part of the Bible is this: What is the literary form of this passage? Find out as much as you can about the different genres that are found in the Bible, not overlooking the smaller ones.
2. Read some of the hymns and songs that you use in worship in your church. How are words used in these? What associations and emotions do they call up? How do you understand the images they use: e.g.

Zion; the dungeon flamed with light; hands that flung stars into space; the early dew of morning/ has passed away at noon?

3. When you read biblical narratives make sure you read to the end of the episode. Think in terms of the whole story rather than individual verses that strike you. Learn to see the details as parts of the whole rather than overlooking the whole because of interesting or helpful details.

4. In reading the Bible ask yourself why the writer has written as he has done. What clues has he left as to his intentions and the things he considers important?

5. When reading prophecy start with what the message meant to its first readers; what functions did the prophet intend his message to perform? What continuing relevance do these have? Are there indications that the prophecy goes beyond the time and context in which it was originally given?

6. Think about your use of words in ordinary speech and the ways in which misunderstandings occur in conversation. What light does this throw on understanding the Bible?

To think about or discuss

Consider Isaiah 35. What is its literary form? What background should it be understood against? What is it actually talking about? What is its fulfilment ?

Where do you think the narrative begun in Acts 12:1 ends? What narrative features can you see here? How does the way it is written make it more dramatic and interesting?

Part III
The world in front of the text

In the first section we recognized that the world out of which the text came is a very different world from our own. To understand a text like Psalm 23 as fully as possible we have to get to know the background which it reflects. Now we come to consider our own world, and ourselves as readers in it.

It is all too easy, as we saw, to think of the ancient world in terms of our own, so we need to take account of ways in which our world is different. We have thought, also, of the importance of the text, but when the Bible is simply shut and unread the text accomplishes nothing. Understanding and interpretation take place when a person reads the text and interacts with it. This means that we have to think about ourselves. What presuppositions do we bring to the Bible? What are our reasons for reading it? What expectations do we have as we read it? These things may easily affect what we understand the Bible to mean.

If we are going to understand the Bible correctly, what helps are there available to us? Are we just on our own when it comes to interpretation? We are promised the help of the Holy Spirit, but in what ways does he help us? Are there any more answers than the ones we have seen? Then there is another important issue. If our world is different from the world out of which the Bible came, it isn't always going to be easy to apply the Bible to today. Can the Bible say very much to our technological world? Can it speak to the complex ethical issues that have arisen because of advances in science and medicine, for example? We have to remember also that there are considerable variations in culture within the modern world. Is the way we see the Bible appropriate for people in, say, South America or India, which are themselves large areas with wide geographical and cultural variation? These are important questions, but they haven't always been given sufficient attention.

Finally, we look on a completed Bible, whereas most of the people to whom its books were written were not in that position. What is it that unites its different books into a whole? The golden thread that binds the Bible into one, and which finds full expression in the New Testament is the person and work of our Lord Jesus Christ. We will conclude by looking at Jesus Christ in all the Scriptures.

Standing back

The claim of the Bible is that it is the Word of God and remains so for ever. It contains the completed revelation of God, and is valid and relevant right up to the time of the return of Jesus Christ. This is the clear implication of verses like this: 'For you have been born again, not of perishable seed, but of imperishable, through the living and enduring Word of God … the word of the Lord stands for ever' (1 Peter 1:23–24). 'All Scripture is God-breathed and is useful for teaching, rebuking, correcting and training in righteousness, so that the man of God may be thoroughly equipped for every good work' (2 Timothy 3:16–17). Jesus said, 'Heaven and earth will pass away, but my words will never pass away' (Mark 13:31).

It is worth remembering, particularly with the 2 Timothy quotation in mind, that Jesus and the apostles used the Old Testament as the Word of God for them. It is true that far greater changes have taken place in the world during the 2,000 years between the New Testament era and today than in the period between Abraham and Jesus. Nevertheless the world that Jesus knew was different from the world of the patriarchs, and different again from the world Israel knew in Egypt, or later in the promised land. Yet he looked upon the whole Old Testament as the Word of God for his day, and we can do the same. Nevertheless, we must think carefully as we read.

Psalm 23 is very familiar to many Christians, and the picture of sheep and their shepherd is accessible even to urban dwellers, so it does not seem unduly strange. But there are parts of the Bible where we seem to be on unfamiliar ground. Even in that psalm we saw that when we reach *You anoint my head with oil* we suddenly find something quite outside our experience. There are many other passages like that. For example, there is the rather surprising incident in which Naomi tells Ruth to go and sleep at Boaz's feet (Ruth 3:1ff.). More generally, modern readers often feel uncomfortable with the war and bloodshed that we come across in the Old Testament. When we think about the violence that frequently makes the news in our own newspapers, and the wars that that are still going on in many parts of the world we begin to get this into perspective. What it shows us is that God has been involved with people as they go through all the varied experiences that come in a fallen world. And that is a comforting thought.

The danger of assuming too readily that the world of the Bible is just like our own is real. In fact if we are going to understand the Bible properly we will need to practise what we might call distancing ourselves from what we are reading. Distancing ourselves means standing back and noticing the differences between our world and the one we are reading about. Someone has said, 'The past is a different country, they do things differently there', and there is a great deal of truth in this statement. As Christians we can find distancing disconcerting because we are used to applying what we read directly to ourselves. However, in the long run it is valuable because it helps us put things into context, it sharpens our awareness of what the text is actually saying, and it enables us to make more accurate and pertinent applications.

Think again of Naomi, Ruth and Boaz in Ruth 3. Reading on into chapter 4 and cross referencing will show us that what was being asked of Boaz was what is known as levirate marriage, where a brother took a widowed sister-in-law in order to raise up an heir to his brother (see Deuteronomy 25:5–10). This seems to have been extended in this case from a brother to the nearest male relative. The actual procedure proposed to Ruth by Naomi should not be understood in terms from our own rural past. Nor should it be understood in terms of pagan behaviour at harvest time, nor any expression of sinfulness amongst the Israelites (note Ruth 2:9). Verse 10 rules these out. At the same time it could easily have been misunderstood (Ruth 2:14) and the passage reflects a concern to establish the propriety of what was done in spite of possible appearances. What we have is an extension of a biblical provision and a custom that is not attested anywhere else.

While it would clearly be a mistake to make any direct application to marriage today, once we have drawn that conclusion we can then begin to work out what can be applied to ourselves. It is intriguing, for example, to note the role played by Naomi here and the way in which the issue was put to Boaz. We could notice also that God's people have to live with the customs of their own day, and need wisdom and sensitivity in doing so conscientiously before God.

It is not just that the Bible might appear strange to us in various passages. We have to recognize that our thought patterns are often significantly different from those we encounter in the Bible. Our way of thinking has developed over the centuries and is shaped by education, the media and the conventions and presuppositions of our society. Levirate marriage is foreign to us because we do not think of the family unit in the way the Old Testament does, nor is the idea of every family having its inheritance in the land one that is relevant to us. There are many other examples. The idea of the solidarity of the human race as descended from Adam is not one we readily grasp. Covenant is crucial in understanding the way God deals with people, but it is not a concept with which we are generally familiar, because modern western society prizes individualism. Another factor is also important. Christians, in fighting for the truth, have sometimes adopted some of the methods and presuppositions of those they were opposing, and the effects of this have come down to us. Standing back and letting the Bible speak for itself is essential, even when its voice seems unexpected and unusual.

But if distancing is important, we also need to remember that there is much that we have in common with the people of Bible times. Ecclesiastes reminds us that there is nothing new under the sun (1:9) and reading the Bible emphasizes how true this is. Here we have people of the same flesh and blood as ourselves. People of great gift and potential, made in the image of God, yet tragically flawed by sin. In spite of the differences we can identify with so much that is described in the Bible.

In particular we remember that spiritual men wrote the Bible under the inspiration of the Holy Spirit. All Christians are born again by the same Spirit and he lives within us. This means that there is a spiritual link between Christians reading the Bible and those who wrote it. And also between them and the God of whom it speaks, and between them and its subject matter. One of the most encouraging and faith-strengthening experiences is to discover the unity we have as Christians with those of very different backgrounds. Many churches have experienced this as believers from other countries have joined them. In spite of our diversity, there is a remarkable oneness. It is just the same when we read the Bible. This is especially our experience when we read the psalms. In spite of the differences of background here are songs and prayers that we can readily identify with. The psalmist's experiences of God and the life of godliness are our experiences; his struggles, hopes and aspirations are ours too.

The reader

Many years ago I was given as a present a small book entitled, *Every Man a Bible Student*. Most churches that I know have a midweek Bible study. Most Christians seem to assume that the Bible needs *studying*. But by and large I have used the word *reader* not *student*. And I have done that deliberately.

Is Psalm 23 first and foremost an object of study? Surely not. Psalm 23 is there to be read, to be enjoyed, to be pondered over. It calls the imagination into play as much as the intellect. Of course it can be studied, and should be studied by those who want to understand it as fully as possible. Nevertheless a psalm yields its meaning primarily to thoughtful, prayerful reading. Job 34:3 says: 'For the ear tests words as the tongue tastes food.' Hearers and readers can get a taste, a sensitivity, to the Bible. We would all agree that the epistles need to be studied to get the most out of them, especially the more doctrinal parts. There is a depth and profundity to the letter to the Romans that requires close attention to the thread of the argument. But they were written as letters, to be read aloud to, and communicate with, the various churches (or individuals) to which they were sent.

Of course close study has its values, but also its dangers. Psalms and letters are intended to be read as wholes. There is always the possibility of missing the wood for the trees. We generally divide the Bible up in our reading, which means we are in danger of losing the continuity of the whole. There are times when it is valuable to read a whole book at one sitting, or with some of the longer books, over a relatively short period of time. That way we can appreciate the aim of the author. Preachers often divide up a passage into headings, or truths, but the effect may be that the impact of the whole is lost. A poem, or narrative, may be reduced to a series of doctrinal propositions. These are then discussed in a purely doctrinal way, sometimes with little or no illustration, application or even reference to the original passage. Study usually involves analysis, but the danger is that after analysing a passage into its component parts it can become difficult to put it back together again. The study of botany may involve dissecting a flower, and this is interesting and important in its way. But it is not the same as Wordsworth seeing a host of golden daffodils in their natural habitat. The glory, beauty and vitality of a flower are lost by analysis through dissection, and there is a danger of doing the same with the Bible.

This is not to denigrate study and scholarship, both are necessary in their place. It is rather to encourage the ordinary reader, if I may use the description. You can utilize the results of scholarship via books, but you can also gain great insight and understanding of God's Word as you read it with prayer and dependence on the Spirit's help.

Respecting the integrity of the text

I came across this sentence in one book: 'A text has no rights except those allowed by the interpreter.' This seems to me absurd, and believing it could lead to a great deal of trouble. The laws of the land, the small print in contracts, the will of a deceased relative all have rights beyond what an interpreter may allow or want to allow. Generally speaking these are all written with great care, they give precise instructions and are intended to rule out debate over what they mean. You can certainly lose out if you don't attend to the small print!

Of course, these are all precise forms of writing that are deliberately intended to exclude ambiguity and to have legal force. But other writers, too, write what they intend and expect to be understood according to what they have said. Good reading respects the text. It comes to it, as far as possible, to listen to what it has to say. It does not come with the purpose of imposing an alien meaning on what is written, nor expecting to be able to add to or stretch the meaning, but to receive it. Of course, with many texts that doesn't mean readers will always agree with what they read. They may disagree strongly, but they disagree because they understand and respect what the text says.

With the Bible we are dealing with the Word of God. Readers who recognize this will take even more care to attend to what is written. They will not jump to conclusions. They will not try to twist what they find to make it fit in with their preconceived ideas of what it ought to say. They will be ready to receive, and believe, what the text says, and to respond to it by obedience.

Preunderstanding

We never approach any piece of writing with a mind that is totally blank. There are things we already know about shepherds and sheep, as we have seen. The trouble is that some of these things may not belong to the world of the text. More than that we may be completely mistaken about something we read. When I read in my church newsletter about Friends and Neighbours I know that this is a gathering for older people, one to which you can invite your friends and neighbours. But to someone else—younger perhaps—Friends and Neighbours could easily be two television programmes.

This is one of the reasons why some people reject the Bible as true, or perhaps why they reinterpret it in ways that are not true to the Bible itself. Such people may come to the Bible already assuming that miracles don't happen, that there are no such beings as evil spirits or angels, and that there is no life beyond this one. It may not be that they are necessarily consciously taking a stand against the Bible, it is simply that their prior understanding of life and reality has no room for these things. Apart from the enlightenment of God's Spirit they are likely to dismiss the Bible without even thinking about it. On the other hand others may come with all sorts of superstitions about spirits. As a result they understand the references to evil spirits according to their beliefs and misunderstand what the Bible has to say. These are fairly extreme examples, but no one comes to the Bible without presuppositions, and these will affect the way it is read and understood. On the one hand we have to try and understand the Bible against its own background. On the other we have to watch out that we do not impose our understanding on it.

Expectations

It is not just that we come to the Bible with our own preunderstanding. Many of us come with our own expectations, also. Those who have been brought up in Christian homes, or who have attended church for a long period of time, frequently expect the Bible to speak to them in certain ways. We have heard the Bible explained—though we might not have fully understood what we heard, or remembered it accurately. We have listened to sermons, we have read the Bible often. All this is very good, and in general is very useful and helpful in understanding what the Bible says. But we must be careful not to take interpretation for granted. We can simply assume where we ought to be giving more careful thought to what is actually written. We naturally tend to understand the Bible in the way it is understood in our church, and we ought not easily to suspect or give up what we have been brought up with. But when all is said and done, the Bible itself is our authority and honesty demands that we read it honestly.

There are people who turn to the Bible to have their own views confirmed. Many of us have a tendency to think that the Bible was written to our agenda and to answer the questions that we have. But it is not as simple as that. Of course, if we are Christians without doubt the Bible will confirm many of our beliefs, and answer many of our questions, but our attitude in coming to it must always be, 'Speak, LORD, for your servant is listening' (1 Samuel 3:9).

At this point we need to reconsider a principle mentioned earlier in the book. Interpreting Scripture by Scripture is undoubtedly a useful and correct procedure. But it must be used with care. There are passages and verses that seem similar but which actually have a different emphasis. We must be careful not to miss the particular point a passage may be making. The Gospel writers may recount the same incident but they do not necessarily have the same purpose in doing so. They all tell the story of Jesus feeding the 5,000, but John shows that this led into a long discourse by Jesus on himself as the bread of life. Matthew, Mark and Luke focus simply on the miracle as a messianic act of compassion and power. John relates the deeper symbolic meaning arising from Jesus' teaching, just as he does with the healing of the man born blind (John 9). The Gospel writers drew their individual portraits of the life, ministry, death and resurrection of Jesus with particular purposes in view. It is important to look at each Gospel in its own right, rather than simply seeking to harmonize them.

Reasons for reading

Do you assume that all readers of the Bible read it for the same reason, perhaps simply to find out what it says? Bible readers are diverse and read it for many different reasons. Most read it devotionally. That is to say, they read a passage as a means of communion with God, looking for some teaching, encouragement, guidance or help from it. They expect to learn more of God himself, and to be better able to live for him and serve him from what they read. In doing this they are reading the Bible differently from the way in which they read virtually all other literature.

But even to speak of reading the Bible devotionally is not specific enough. People read the Bible in a devotional way for more than one reason. This often depends on their spiritual condition or their circumstances. Some simply want to learn. Others are looking for a word which will meet their particular need. Some want to recapture a previous sense of God's goodness and nearness which they feel they have lost. Some may be in danger of misusing it by seeking guidance from specific words that they want to apply to themselves that did not have that meaning in the mind of the author.

On a broader front the reasons for reading are as varied as the readers themselves. Some are reading to pass exams; others to prepare a message which they have to speak; others because they are broken in spirit and are desperately searching for a word of truth and light; some are approaching death, some are burdened with a great sense of sin and need; some read formally, because they have always done so. But the point is this. Your reason for reading, and the condition of your mind and heart at the time of reading will influence the way you read, and the way you respond to what you read. There can be no doubt about that.

Think of reading Psalm 23, or hearing it read. How many have come to the psalm in times of illness, or old age, or bereavement, or at the end of their lives! Those who believe, find it comes to them with consoling power and brings peace and quietness into their souls. What is happening here? These are people who are hungering and thirsting for God and reality, for help and encouragement. The evocative power of the text is matched by a receptivity and longing. The words come with a special power because of the particular situation and need of the readers or hearers. This is part of the reason for Psalm 23 finding its place in the Word of God. It is there for the spiritual good of all who read it, but perhaps especially for those who are in one way or another passing through the dark valley. It has the special assurance for them that this shepherd stays with his sheep at such a time.

The practical point is this. Why we read the Bible—the attitude we have, the condition of our hearts, our desires and intentions—will have an effect on how we read and what we receive from what we have read. The sceptic is unlikely to gain much from reading the Bible; he might in fact find things he believes justify his scepticism—that may be what he's looking for. The casual reader may not be particularly stirred by what she reads. The blinkered reader will see what he wants to see, but may miss much else that would be of help and benefit. There is a particular danger of coming to the Bible for, say, inspiration and comfort, but having our minds closed to its warnings and hard sayings. We do not, of course, always come to the Bible with special reasons for reading, or in special need. We can simply come recognizing that the Bible is God's Word, with a desire honestly and humbly to listen, receive and respond to what it says.

Mind and heart

Reading is an intellectual exercise—we read sentences which we understand with the mind. But it is not enough to say that. The mind is not a self-contained intellect which simply reasons and thinks. However you describe the mind there is a close link with emotion. John Keats has a poem entitled 'On First Looking into Chapman's Homer', Chapman having translated Homer into English in the seventeenth century. Keats describes his emotions on reading Chapman's book like this:

—Then felt I like some watcher of the skies
When a new planet swims into his ken;
Or like stout Cortez—when with eagle eyes
He stared at the Pacific.

New worlds opened up for him when he read. He felt like someone discovering a new planet, like the first European gazing out over the Pacific ocean. Perhaps few who read this book will have felt like Keats on reading Homer—probably few will have even read Homer or have any intention of reading him! But we can understand that simply reading a book can have a profound emotional effect upon us. It can move us to tears; it can make us laugh out loud; it can stir us to action; it can fill us with joy or make us feel angry. And so we could go on. Not all books have such effects. But some books do and are intended to. By the things they recount and the way in which they are written they can move us deeply.

And so it is with the Bible; especially with the Psalms, and not least among them Psalm 23. And this emotional impact is intended by not only the writers, but also by the divine Author who is behind it all. If one of the members of the church at Corinth, after 2 Corinthians had been read out publicly, had said, 'Well, that was interesting', Paul, had he known, would almost have been in despair. Paul had poured out his heart in that letter: 'We have spoken freely to you, Corinthians, and opened wide our hearts to you ... As a fair exchange—I speak as to my children—open wide your hearts also' (6:11,13). What Paul wanted was an emotional response; a far deeper response than could be indicated by saying, 'That was interesting.'

The response Paul desired was not merely an emotional one, it would also be a truly spiritual one. Paul was writing to the Corinthians as Christians. He was certainly not trying to play on their feelings. He was addressing them with spiritual appeals based on the fact that they were spiritual people, even though, as in his first letter, he could scarcely consider them spiritual (1 Corinthians 3:1–4). We can express it like this. Paul was writing as a spiritual person himself, under the guidance and in the power of the Holy Spirit. He was writing to people who were spiritual—even though they had reverted to an infantile condition—praying, perhaps expecting, that the Spirit would use his words and cause a deeply spiritual response to what he had written.

So, right reading involves a sympathetic attention to what Scripture is saying. It involves the imagination and allows the emotions to be engaged with the text. This is not just going by feelings. It is not simply responding emotionally to a verse or passage without any thought. It is true spiritual feeling arising out of what God says in his Word. The Bible does move us, and is intended to do so. It can sometimes leave us in tears of conviction or repentance. It can lift us up to the heavens with joy unspeakable. It can open up visions of glory to us that take our breath away.

A special impact
Listen to Augustine (354–430):

So was I speaking, and weeping in the most bitter contrition of my heart, when, lo! I heard from a neighbouring house a voice, as of a boy or girl, I know not, chanting, and oft repeating, 'Take up and read; Take up and read.' Instantly, my countenance altered, I began to think most intently, whether children were wont in any kind of play to sing such words: nor could I remember ever to have heard the like. So checking the torrent of my tears, I arose; interpreting it to be no other than a command from God, to open the book, and read the first chapter I should find ... I seized, opened, and in silence read that section, on which my eyes first fell: 'Not in rioting and drunkenness, not in chambering and wantonness, not in strife and envying: but put ye on the Lord Jesus Christ, and make not provision for the flesh,' in concupiscence. No further would I read; nor needed I: for instantly at the end of this sentence, by a light as it were of serenity infused into my heart, all the darkness of doubt vanished away.[1]

Then there is Martin Luther (1483–1546):

I greatly longed to understand Paul's Epistle to the Romans and nothing stood in the way but that one expression, 'the justice of God', because I took it to mean that justice whereby God is just and deals justly in punishing the unjust ... Night and day I pondered until I saw the connection between the justice of God and the statement 'the just shall live by his faith'. Then I grasped that the justice of God is that righteousness by which through grace and sheer mercy God justifies us through faith. Thereupon I felt myself to be reborn and to have gone through open doors into paradise. The words of Scripture took on a new meaning and whereas the 'justice of God' had filled me with hate, now it became to me inexpressibly sweet in greater love. This passage of Paul became to me a gate to heaven.[2]

There is a great similarity between these two quotations, but also a great difference. In Luther's case he was studying the letter to the Romans, wrestling with what it said (especially in 1:17). In Augustine's case when he picked up the Bible he opened it at Romans and read what met his eye (13:13–14). But in both cases the words came home to their hearts with great light and power. For both men these were life-changing experiences; neither was ever the same again. Although Augustine read the first words he saw, these were words completely suited to his condition. He needed to put on Jesus Christ, and to make no provision for the flesh. The experience he had, as Luther also, was one in which the reality of the words of Scripture came home to him. He did put on Jesus Christ; he did renounce opportunities for the flesh—his sinful heart expressing itself through the body—to act in his life. With Luther, it was his understanding that was liberated. He saw what 'the righteousness of God' really meant and it freed him from fear and filled him with joy.

In both cases we must see the Holy Spirit working within them. The truth each needed was there on the page of Scripture, but they needed also an enlightening and liberating work of the Spirit in the heart, that is, in the centre of their inner being, the source of all thinking, feeling and willing. Two further elements seem to be here. First, the very distress each was in, though different in nature, was already an evidence of the Holy Spirit at work. Secondly, we ought not to think of the work of the Spirit as separate from Scripture. Both in creating distress and conviction and in bringing faith and salvation, it was Word and Spirit together. The Word coming to the soul as it really is, the living, powerful Word of the present, active Spirit. As Paul explained to the Thessalonians, 'our gospel came to you not simply with words, but also with power, with the Holy Spirit and with deep conviction' (1 Thessalonians 1:5).

What we have here are special cases of the way in which God speaks to our hearts through his Word. There is a particular power and clarity about these experiences. People have similar experiences today, experiences that are dramatic and life-transforming, but in general these are exceptional, just as they were in the past. It may be that both these are cases of conversion, and God may still convert in similar fashion today. But God may also speak very powerfully to those who are already believers and make great changes in their lives in a short period. In reading the Bible we must be ready for God to speak by his Spirit. Whether in a still small voice, or with a voice of power, or with sudden illumination, the Spirit speaks the Word to us. However it comes, we are to receive it and obey it.

He leads me ... and guides me

But how does he lead and guide? The *picture* is clear enough. The shepherd goes in front of the sheep and the sheep follow, whether to quiet waters, along the right paths, or through the valley of the shadow of death. But how does the Lord lead and guide his human sheep, and especially how does he lead and guide through the Bible?

Some things are straightforward. The Lord leads by the way he directs and overrules our lives. We are usually brought into and through the dark valley simply in the course of living, not by being given special instructions to go into it. Clearly God guides by his commands, by principles we can see in the Bible and by the examples that are recorded for us. The example of Jesus himself provides a guide for us to follow. It is true that later we shall have to think about the way we are to transpose Bible principles into the present day, but that is a problem of application.

Perhaps the real problem can be best posed by giving some examples. If I am seriously ill and worried about my condition and read John 11:4 and the words of Jesus seem to come to me with special force, 'This sickness will not end in death' can I take them as a promise to myself? Suppose I am troubled about a big decision and there are several alternatives before me. I am inclined to take one and read, 'Whether you turn to the right or to the left, your ears will hear a voice behind you saying, "This is the way, walk in it"' (Isaiah 30:21). Can I take that as indicating that what I am inclined to is God's way for me? Or if I feel particularly weak and ineffective as a Christian and read in Joshua 1:6, 'Be strong and courageous', is that a direct word for me?

Taking the last example first the answer is, 'Yes, certainly.' Whether these words appear to come with special force or not, they are a general encouragement, not just to Joshua, but to all God's covenant people, and are repeated throughout Scripture (see, for example, 1 Corinthians 16:13). With the first two examples, and others like them, be very careful. Many, many Christians through the centuries have been misled and disappointed by taking verses as a personal message to them in a particular situation. Moreover, the first two examples take the words right out of their context. But in spite of that I'm not sure that there aren't ways of thinking through verses like this and finding that they may give special help. Let me give a personal example.

The evening before I was due to see a hospital specialist I read Psalm 112. When I came to the words, 'He will have no fear of bad news; his heart is steadfast, trusting the LORD' (verse 7), my instinctive reaction was, 'Is this preparing me for bad news'? Paradoxically the verse made me apprehensive about what I might hear next day, instead of having no fear! As I thought about it, however, I realized that trusting in the Lord, my heart could be steadfast, and the verse stayed with me as I went in the morning. As it happened the news was neither bad nor good, it depended on further tests. Two biopsies and one small operation later the news was good. So God cannot have been telling me through the verse that bad news awaited me, but it was still very valuable for me to have my attention particularly drawn to it.

There are three elements here. There is my own thinking through the verse, what it meant and how it might apply to me. Then there is the way in which the verse functioned in my own experience. There was an interaction in my own consciousness between the words of Scripture and the events as they took place. This is something very important. It is an inward, spiritual application of the Word of God in actual life. Then, finally, there is the fact that my attention was initially drawn to that verse. How did this come about? The fact that I was already aware that the news could be bad, probably meant I inevitably focussed on that. So it was my own heightened sense of the situation that led me to notice that verse in particular. But was God entirely outside of that process? And was that verse actually irrelevant to my situation? No—in both cases. In fact, God was at work all the time and it was his Word that I read, and I came to see its proper relevance to me.

Let me try to clarify this with another illustration. I know an elderly lady who had lived on her own after her husband's death for many years. In her nineties this verse came powerfully to her mind—I'm not sure whether it was as she read the passage or whether it seemed to come out of the blue: 'When you were younger you dressed yourself and went where you wanted; but when you are old you will stretch out your hands, and someone else will dress you and lead you where you do not want to go' (John 21:18). Not long after this her health deteriorated and she was no longer able to care for herself adequately and she went into a residential home. She is sure that the Lord prepared her for this by that verse. There is no doubt that it played a very significant part in enabling an independent-minded lady to be reconciled to leaving the home she loved and going where she would much rather not be.

Here is a verse in which Jesus spoke very specifically to Peter and which Scripture itself applies to the way in which he was going to glorify God by death. It certainly doesn't mean that a particular lady at the turn of the twenty-first century was going to go into residential care. But it is not adequate to leave it there. The verse *does* remind us that there are occasions in life when, in God's providence, believers may be taken by others into places they would rather not go. It is also true that in later life people may become dependent on others and have to live in circumstances and places which are not their preference. I do not find it surprising that, in her circumstances, this verse alerted her to the possibility that the sort of change which was on its way would take place. Nor do I think that a gracious God had nothing to do with her being prepared in this way. I do not understand her experience in quite the way she does, but I do believe that God used that verse to make her submissive to a change which was to come in her life. Peter had to submit to a change, though a different one, one which would actually bring his life to an end, and so had she.

Neither of these examples required any definite action to be taken. It was rather a matter of waiting to see how things turned out. In the second example it might have been the case that the lady had remained in her own home until the Lord took her in death. However, in some cases people feel that God is telling them to take a certain action through a verse, or perhaps a passage, that they have read. For numbers of missionaries their call, and all that resulted from it, seems to have come like that. This was probably so for some who served God faithfully for many years in very difficult circumstances with great self-sacrifice. But it was probably also the case for others who came home after one term of service or even less than that, and never returned. Sincere Christians can get themselves into considerable trouble through following what they believe a verse is saying to them.

This is not the place to deal with this question in full, for this is a discussion of how God speaks through the Bible, not of the call to various forms of Christian service. Three things can be said, however. Firstly, knowing that we can be mistaken about what we believe to be the voice of God—knowing also that Satan himself can use Scripture (Matthew 4:5–6)—it is right to check and test what we believe Scripture is saying to us personally (1 Thessalonians 5:21). To think things through prayerfully and carefully; to examine what the text says and what its context is; to consider other similar passages, is always wise and right. Secondly, and to anticipate a further discussion, while we rejoice that faith is a personal thing, it is also true that much of the Bible is written to God's people corporately. We are not simply Christians in isolation; our understanding of God's Word develops and deepens in the fellowship of the church (consider Philippians 3:15–17). And the call to ministry is itself a church matter (Acts 13:1–3). All these considerations mean that a call to missionary service needs to be prayerfully evaluated within the context of the church and not simply in an individualistic way.

Thirdly, general circumstances should be taken into account as well. Do your circumstances and the way God has ordered your life up to the present suggest that he is pointing towards the direction you now believe you should take? Prayerful reflection is always more important than jumping to conclusions.

Interpretation

We are still thinking about the reader, but we are now going to think about him or her in a way that is more controversial. We have thought of the effect the Bible can have upon a reader, but what about what the reader brings to the Bible? Here we are going beyond preunderstanding and expectations. Do readers simply receive or do they contribute? In the act of understanding do they bring their own contribution to interpretation? I know what I said earlier about respecting the text, but there are certainly texts that require—indeed, invite—the active co-operation of the reader and this is true of a great deal of the Bible.

Consider Psalm 93 this time. The Psalm begins by celebrating the kingship of the Lord and the stability of the world which this implies. But in verse 3 there is a sudden change,

'The seas have lifted up, O LORD,
the seas have lifted up their voice;
the seas have lifted up their pounding waves.'

The question is, what does the psalmist mean by 'the seas' (or 'floods')? Here is a metaphor, but to what does it refer? It is possible that the psalmist has some particular trouble in view, and he calls out to God as he thinks of it, but even if he is thinking in more general terms he leaves it to us, the readers, to supply our own understanding. We could think of 'the seas' as referring to all that challenges God's sovereignty, or more particularly to Israel's enemies, or to the psalmist's enemies, or to adverse circumstances, or to temptations and sins, or the powers of darkness. What we have here is audio-visual. In our mind's-eye we are to see the threatening, crashing billows, and hear the thunder of waves breaking on the shore. We then transfer that to those things which threaten our own safety and peace, looking back to see that the Lord on high is mightier than all the breakers that pound our life's shore.

There is no need to say more about metaphor as this has already been considered earlier. But it is not only poetry or metaphor that calls on the reader to make a contribution. The same is often true with parables. From one point of view the parables of Jesus tend to challenge the attitudes and beliefs of his hearers, particularly the scribes, or law-teachers, and the Pharisees. But they also invite us to consider them carefully. Their meaning is not always on the surface, at least as far as modern, western people are concerned, and they repay prayerful consideration.

Consider what we know as the parable of the good Samaritan (Luke 10:25–37). There are, I think, several lessons that our Lord was making here, though I am not sure I have read any interpretation that fully satisfies me. Clearly the most important point is that the one who took pity on the wounded man was a Samaritan, someone who was despised by Jews both as of mixed race and heretical in doctrine. But notice how the parable proceeds. A priest comes down the road and passes by. Then a Levite does the same. Who would the law-teacher expect next after a priest and Levite if not a teacher of the law, one like himself? You can almost see him anticipating that is what Jesus is going to say. This would be the point of the story. The teacher of the law has pity on the man, thus setting an example and answering the question, 'Who is my neighbour?' and showing the actual law-teacher what he was to do. But Jesus' parable takes a breath-taking turn, leaving the law-keeper—and us—wondering why he introduced a Samaritan. So think carefully about what Jesus said. That surely is what he intends us to do.

I have already pointed out that the New Testament letters, while mainly consisting of teaching, are letters first of all designed, in most cases, to be read out to the churches to which they were addressed. Only secondarily do they become objects of study. As we read, or hear them, our minds need to be active as well as receptive. Ephesians 3:17–19 contains one of Paul's prayers for the Ephesians. 'And I pray that you, being rooted and established in love, may have power, together with all the saints, to grasp how wide and long and high and deep is the love of Christ, and to know this love that surpasses knowledge—that you may be filled to the measure of all the fullness of God.' How did Paul hope those who heard would respond to this? Not, surely, by saying, 'Here is Paul praying and this is what he prays.' Rather to hear, or read, this prayer would have moved the Ephesians to deep thankfulness for such a prayer, and a longing to experience what was prayed for. And more. They would surely have entered into that prayer; made it their own; sought the help of the Holy Spirit to grasp and to know, in some measure, the love of Christ. And that is how we are to read it.

As we read, our minds, imaginations and emotions are to be alert. There is an inter-action between the words we read and our own psychic processes. What we read suggests associations, enlarges understanding, moves our hearts and engages us actively. The text is still supreme, and we have to filter out what, on reflection, is inappropriate or not sustained by it. But our knowledge and understanding, our enjoyment and responsiveness, grow and are enlarged.

Notes on Chapter 15

1 **St Augustine,** *Confessions,* trans. **E.B. Pusey** (London, J.M. Dent & Co., n.d.), p. 170–1.
2 Quoted in **Roland Bainton,** *Here I Stand* (New York, Mentor Books, 1950), p. 49–50).

The church

So far we have been presupposing a sort of triangular relationship in reading the Bible. There is the text, written by the human author. There is the reader, and then there is God, who by his Holy Spirit caused the author to write as he did, and also works in the mind and heart of the reader. But the situation is not as simple as that. Some Christians seem to think only in these terms, but it is too individualistic a way of looking at things. The world in front of the text includes 2,000 years and more of history, and the Christian reader belongs to the church of the Lord Jesus Christ and ought, unless this is not possible, to belong to a local congregation. What bearing does this have on reading the Bible?

The church and the Holy Spirit

Before answering that question it would be valuable to think about the relationship between the church and the Holy Spirit. We know that the Spirit indwells each Christian: 'You, however, are controlled not by the sinful nature but by the Spirit, if the Spirit of God lives in you. And if anyone does not have the Spirit of Christ, he does not belong to Christ' (Romans 8:9). However, it is also true that the Holy Spirit lives in the people of God corporately. In Ephesians 2:21–22 Paul writes: 'In him [Christ] the whole building is joined together and rises to become a holy temple in the Lord. And in him you too are being built together to become a dwelling in which God lives by his Spirit.' And in 1 Corinthians 3:16–17: 'Don't you know that you yourselves are God's temple and that God's Spirit lives in you? If anyone destroys God's temple, God will destroy him; for God's temple is sacred, and you are that temple.'

Down through the centuries the Holy Spirit has lived within the true church of Jesus Christ. He has been guiding it, empowering it, making it holy, leading it into all truth. He is still doing the same today. He lives and works within each local church, too, and we must recognize this corporate dimension in the Holy Spirit's ministry. It would be presumptuous, perhaps even sinful, to ask the Holy Spirit to teach us and help us in understanding the Bible, and at the same time to ignore what he has shown to godly servants down through the centuries. Even worse would be to despise what others have written, to set it aside as 'book learning' and imagine that the Spirit must reveal everything in a personal, individual, immediate way. To return to Paul's prayer in Ephesians 3:16ff.: 'I pray that out of his glorious riches he may strengthen you with power through his Spirit in your inner being … that you … may have power, together with all the saints, to grasp how wide and long and high and deep is the love of Christ, and to know this love that surpasses knowledge …' We learn and know, not just on our own and by ourselves, but 'together, with all the saints'.

Pastors and teachers

In his commission to the apostles, and to the succeeding churches, Jesus included 'teaching them to obey everything I have commanded you' (Matthew 28:20). Disciples were to be baptised, bringing them into fellowship with each other in the church. And the church has a teaching commission, so that the lives of Jesus' disciples may be conformed to the pattern he has given. In Ephesians 4:11–13 we read that the ascended Christ: 'gave … some to be pastors and teachers, to prepare God's people for works of service, so that the body of Christ may be built up until we all reach unity in the faith and in the knowledge of the Son of God and become mature, attaining to the whole measure of the fullness of Christ.' Understanding the Bible was never intended to happen apart from the teaching ministry which Jesus Christ has instituted in the churches.

This puts a great responsibility on those who are called to this work. They have to do their best to present themselves to God as those who are approved, workmen who do not need to be ashamed because they correctly handle the word of truth (see 2 Timothy 2:15). There are at least two aspects here. Firstly, those who teach must do so in such a way that those who listen can see that they are dealing faithfully and accurately with the Bible. They must take care, not only to preach biblically, but to let it be seen that the passages they are expounding are actually saying what they are saying. Secondly, by preaching in this way they will be setting a pattern for their hearers to read and understand the Bible for themselves. There is a style of preaching which tends to make the hearers say, 'I could never get out of the Bible the things which he does!' Far better is the style which leads the hearers to say, 'Oh, yes; I can see how the Bible is saying that.'

Teachers have the opportunity of studying the Bible systematically and carefully. They will build up resources that enable them to explore the world behind the text, and determine, as far as possible, the correct translation and its meaning. Their responsibilities are great. There is no doubt that their hearers will follow their example in interpreting the Bible, consciously and unconsciously. So let them preach in a way that encourages and enables their hearers to read their Bibles more intelligently and to gain the maximum from doing so.

The converse of this is that churches need to ensure, as far as is possible, that a real teaching and preaching ministry is a vital part of their life. I almost want to say 'teaching through preaching' because I want to avoid the idea of ministry which simply informs—a lecturing style which does not grip the heart, which does not feel and express the pulse of the biblical writers. A ministry without passion is bound to be unfaithful to the Bible, because there is much passionate writing in it. At the same time it has to be said that just as the biblical writers have their own personalities, so do those who preach it. A preaching style needs to be authentic to the personality of the preacher, as well as true to the text and its author. There is bound to be variation among preachers. Just as God uses the individuality and personality of the biblical writers, so he also uses the different personalities and strengths of those who preach.

To return to the point, however, churches need to call, to help equip, and to receive gladly, at least one preaching teacher. If he is to fulfil his responsibilities he will need books and will want to keep abreast of the most valuable that are being currently published. He will find help and encouragement through conferences and opportunities to study more thoroughly. The church that understands these things and enables its minister to give himself to the work to which he has been called will find it benefits greatly.

Interpretation over the centuries

Bible interpretation is not a modern discipline, nor is the teaching ministry of the Holy Spirit restricted to any one period in the church's history. From the very beginning, with the apostles setting the pattern with their treatment of the Old Testament, God's people have sought to understand his Word. There are undoubtedly periods of particular significance for biblical interpretation, but having said that, we have to realize that we are heirs of all the thought and prayers that have produced the various commentaries and sermons that have been preserved for posterity. It would be foolish to think that we can learn nothing from the past, that the present generation of biblical scholars has got everything right, and that there is no need to consult any other. Neither must we simply settle on the Puritan era, or the Reformation, or the early church fathers as the only source of correct interpretation. The fact is that we can learn from them all, and where they all tend to agree we can be reasonably sure that is the correct understanding. Some of the most helpful commentaries are those which summarize and popularize the common understanding of most Christians down through the centuries.

Biblical scholarship

Some Christians tend to look with suspicion on scholarship. This is understandable because there is no doubt that some scholars have been opponents of the full inspiration of the Bible, and have been in the lead in casting doubt on much that it says. This is not, however, because they have been scholars, but because they have been unbelieving scholars, or scholars who have been unduly influenced by secular presuppositions. The Christian church has always been dependent on scholarship—though, of course, not on scholarship alone. It was Jewish scholars who translated the Old Testament into Greek and provided the people of our Lord's day with a text they could understand. Similarly most of us have to use translations of the Bible into English, and we should be very thankful for the dependable translations that are available for us. Only a very few are able to read Hebrew and Greek as easily as they read English, and these are—scholars! We are also indebted to those who have provided commentaries on the biblical books, and who have written about the culture of Bible times. There are many excellent books that cast a flood of light upon the Bible.

The fact is that scholarship is simply diligent, careful research. It is true, of course, that those who spend their lives in scholarly pursuits—

researching, teaching, writing—are usually very gifted intellectually. But every Christian, and every minister, ought to read and study the Bible with care, integrity and thoroughness. Shallow thinking, jumping to conclusions, careless reading which disregards what the Bible actually says, Scripture twisting, ought never to be marks of true Christians. We may not be scholars ourselves, but we recognize the value of scholarship. We try to understand the Bible as honestly and carefully as we are able within our own limitations. And we are thankful that down through the centuries the Lord has raised up those whom he has gifted to enable us to understand his Word better, and is still doing so. We acknowledge, too, that some who are not Christian believers may yet give accurate information about, for example, the biblical languages, and that professedly Christian scholars who do not accept the full inspiration of Scripture can nevertheless often write with integrity about what Scripture means. In this area, as in others, we are to 'test everything' and 'hold on to the good' (1 Thessalonians 5:21).

New perspectives

Although in the early centuries the Christian faith spread throughout the Mediterranean world, with strong churches in Turkey, east of Palestine and northern Africa, we ourselves are to a large extent heirs of the great European Christian tradition, especially that springing from the Reformation. For nearly two centuries Christianity has been in decline in Europe and this tradition is now at its strongest in the United States. The growth areas of Christianity are in South America, Africa and the Far East. People from these areas of the world are coming to look at the Bible with fresh eyes. Some of them are in cultures or life situations that are closer to those of the early believers, and they are therefore able to understand some parts of the Bible better than we are. They feel its power and relevance in ways that we do not. We have to be prepared to learn from them.

It is true that in some cases Christians from other cultures are over-influenced by beliefs and attitudes that lead to distortion of the biblical message. But we too are heirs to a way of thinking that has been heavily influenced by philosophical ideas that are alien to biblical truth. Consequently we may find that Christians without the cultural and intellectual baggage that we bring to the Bible may help us much more than we anticipate. Many new Christians are subject to persecution similar to the early days of Christianity, while we are not. They have come to faith and have to live their lives in clearly non-Christian societies in a way that is not yet true for us. They are not embarrassed by supernaturalism, and have not been brought up in a rationalistic atmosphere, but the same is not the case for us. They have to apply the Bible directly to problems we do not share, and are called to adopt lifestyles that are more radically different from their non-Christian neighbours. For all these reasons we can look forward to a far greater input to biblical interpretation from those parts of the world in days to come.

Understanding and obedience in the local church

To return to the local church. It isn't only that teachers and preachers interpret the Word of God for their hearers. There is more to it than that. Firstly, there is an interaction within the church which helps those who preach to do so effectively. Preachers learn from their congregations. People in diverse situations come to the Bible with different questions and obtain different insights, and wise preachers learn from these. There are things we cannot learn from books on interpretation that we can learn from our fellow members. It is at least partly for this reason that a place for discussion needs to be found within the church. We do not have time to talk to everyone individually in the church, but times of open discussion enable everyone who wishes to, to make a contribution. Part of the purpose of this book is to enable members to make more useful contributions within their own fellowships.

It is because of this interaction that many preachers develop a particular rapport between their own congregation and themselves. When a man preaches to his own congregation he is preaching to people he knows, to people he converses with, and whose situation is known. He is likely to know quite well, perhaps very well, those with problems and difficulties. He is able to make his sermons relevant, applicatory and suited to his hearers in a way he cannot when he is preaching somewhere else.

Secondly, there is a real sense in which the effectiveness of preaching is seen in the way in which it is lived out by the church. The church should be growing in understanding, developing biblical priorities and attitudes, changing in its life as a church and in the lives of the individual members. Different pictures have been used to try and illustrate this point. There is the picture of an orchestra and its conductor. The preacher is the conductor, the Bible is the score, and the orchestra is the congregation who 'play' according to the interpretation of the score by the conductor and produce a harmonious and melodious life together. Another illustration is that of a coach and a sports team, perhaps player-coach best fits the bill. The coach guides and enables the team to play together at their best; and he himself is part of the team, playing by the same rules, presenting a pattern to the rest of the team. This idea seems quite clear in Philippians 3:15–17: 'All of us who are mature should take such a view of things. And if on some point you think differently, that too God will make clear to you. Only let us live up to what we have already attained. Join with others in following my example, brothers, and take note of those who live according to the pattern we gave you.'

This is the ideal of interpretation. The Bible being explained and applied by those who preach in such a way that the whole congregation of God's people receives its truth and lives out what it says. And this taking place not just because one or perhaps two are able to interpret for the rest, but those who interpret also gain insight and understanding by their mutual fellowship within the church. One writer says this: 'It is my contention that the final goal of hermeneutics is … the sermon.'[1] But I want to go beyond that. Another writer says: 'The priesthood of all believers is not individualistic; it is something we hold in common with all believers. We interpret Scripture together. We serve each other by exchanging ideas in the hope that the Spirit will orchestrate our individual contributions into a symphony of understanding'.[2] And not just a symphony of understanding, but a symphony of living. Understanding leading to renewed behaviour in every area of life. Glory to God in the church (Ephesians 3:21)!

Notes

1 **Grant Osborne,** *The Hermeneutical Spiral* (Leicester, IVP, 1997), p. 12.
2 **Richard Pratt,** *He Gave Us Stories* (Phillipsburg, N.J., Presbyterian & Reformed, 1993), p. 69.

Application

The Bible is not only to be read—it is to be applied to our lives. One of the values of the preaching ministry is just this; it applies the Word to us. When we read the Bible on our own it is all too easy to apply what we read in ways that suit us and evade more challenging applications. When we hear it preached, applications are made that we cannot avoid without disobedience.

We need to understand application in as broad a way as possible. The Bible impacts on our hearts and lives in many different ways, and in different ways at different times. The Bible makes us 'wise for salvation'. It applies to our spiritual lives and the condition of our souls before God. It teaches us truth that we need to know; about God, ourselves, and God's way with us, both in saving us, guiding us, making us holy and getting us ready for heaven. It has to be applied to every area of our life and behaviour: to work, to living in the home, to marriage and parenthood, to our relationships, to our finances, to our ambitions and goals. We are to look at our circumstances and the things that come to us in the light of what the Bible teaches us.

Most Christians are generally more concerned about its application to their own personal lives and circumstances than to anything else. But much of the Bible was originally written to Israel, or to churches, rather than to individuals. So we need to apply what the Bible says to our church life, to our worship and work together, and to the general condition of Christians in our own church, area and country today. In many cases application is not difficult—though bringing our lives into conformity with what the Bible says may be. But there are areas of difficulty, and we consider some of these.

Applying the Bible to today

An obvious question arises when we read the Old Testament. How are we to apply it to today? There are actually two questions here. The Old Testament was written to the nation of Israel, God's chosen nation. So how do we apply what was said to God's people as a nation, in days when the nation has been replaced by the church? God's church is not to be identified now with any one nation or race of people. Christians belong to many nations and are a minority in all of them. Secondly, how do we apply God's law as revealed in the Old Testament? The two questions are not the same, but they are very closely linked.

The most usual answer given to the second question is to distinguish between moral, ceremonial and national commandments. Moral laws are always binding—'You shall not steal' (Exodus 20:15). Ceremonial laws are fulfilled in Jesus Christ, and done away with by his coming—see Mark 7:18–19: '"Don't you see that nothing that enters a man from the outside can make him 'unclean'? For it doesn't go into the heart but into his stomach, and then out of his body." (In saying this, Jesus declared all foods "clean".)' National laws only applied to Israel during the Old Testament period.

This way of looking at things has been criticized in at least two ways. One criticism is that the Bible itself doesn't draw any distinctions like this between the commands. This is only partly true, and the distinctions are there in the nature of the case. Some commands *are* moral, some ceremonial and some national. Then it is also pointed out that some laws have both moral and ceremonial elements, or elements of all three. The fifth commandment says, 'Honour your father and your mother, so that you may live long in the land the Lord your God is giving you' (Exodus 20:12). If the first part of the law is moral, the second half is national—'in the land the Lord your God is giving you'. However, that didn't prevent the apostle Paul from quoting this commandment and applying it to Gentile children at Ephesus, even expanding the promise so that he says, 'that it may go well with you and that you may enjoy long life on the earth' (Ephesians 6:2–3).

My own view is that the division into moral, ceremonial and national is useful as a general rule and will prevent serious mistakes. However, national laws and ceremonial laws may enshrine important principles and need to be considered carefully. The way Paul handles the fifth commandment shows us that, and is a valuable pointer to the way we can apply Old Testament laws. More will be said about Israel as a nation further on.

A more general question about application is relevant to both Testaments. The Bible was written to people whose culture and customs were very different from our own. Are some of the commands and instructions so related to that culture that they cannot be simply transferred to the present? It certainly appears so. An obvious example is found in 1 Corinthians 11:2–16. In that passage Paul says that women should have their heads covered (some understand the word to refer to hair which has been done up) when praying or prophesying, which is often taken to mean 'during worship'. As a result women in the past used to attend church wearing hats. Some have argued strenuously for continuing the practice of women covering their heads. When I was young I often passed a church building which had three large notices on the three sides visible from the road, 'Women and girls attending this church must have their heads covered'! Nowadays it is much more generally held that Paul is reflecting a situation in which for a woman to appear uncovered would be immodest and dishonour her husband. That was the case in that culture, it is argued—and we can think of cultures today of which this would still be true—but as it is not so in our culture we have to apply what Paul says in a different way. One of the interesting things is that some who argued most strongly against this cultural understanding had already made a cultural shift themselves. They applied Paul's words to women wearing hats— objects of adornment designed to enhance a woman's appearance—rather than to wearing a veil, which is quite different.

What makes this an urgent matter is the fact that the cultural argument is being used to challenge quite a number of practices which churches have generally believed to be biblical. For example, it is used with regard to women's ministry. The ministry of women, it is said, would have offended against the cultural preferences of those days, but it no longer does so in these days, so in our situation we do not need to be bound by what the Bible says. A similar argument has been used to justify homosexual practice. What needs to be done in cases like these is to consider *all* the evidence the Bible gives us. For example, Paul bases what he says about women not being permitted to teach or have authority over a man on the fact that Adam was formed first, and the woman was deceived (1 Timothy 2:11–15). So the reasons given are creational and theological, not merely cultural.

Some instructions surely are culturally or circumstantially conditioned: the covered head (or properly done hair), the holy kiss, to stop drinking water only and using a little wine (1 Timothy 5:23). This last example is merely circumstantial; it was the condition of water in those days that led Paul to give his advice to Timothy. But even where an instruction is culturally conditioned, it is not enough to leave it at that. We need to look at the principle behind the command and see what application that has to us. Jesus told his disciples when they went out to preach the kingdom not to take money or an extra tunic 'for the worker is worthy of his keep'. In the Jewish society of Jesus' day itinerant preachers would have been given hospitality by those they spoke to. This, however, would not be the case today in many cultures, including our own. But the principle is still valid. Evangelists will usually need to take money with them, but they do not necessarily have to work for it in some other employment. Fellow believers who recognize that Christian workers are 'worthy of keep' can provide it. Similarly, even if we do not greet fellow believers with a kiss, we certainly do need to express warm recognition and welcome to brothers and sisters in the Lord.

Seeking solutions to today's dilemmas from the Bible

If there are difficulties when we start with the Bible and try to apply it to today, there is also the opposite difficulty. If we start with today's questions the problems seem even greater. How can we use the Bible to guide our lives when conditions are so very different from Bible times, and when many of the greatest dilemmas arise from medical and scientific advances only recently made? We need to be cautious here. We have to recognize that many Christians in the past went badly wrong, and we need to try and ensure that we don't make similar mistakes. The time was when Christians thought it was wrong to make things easier for women in childbirth because this was to undermine God's Word in Genesis 3:16. Paul's words in Romans 'Owe no man anything' (13:8, Authorized Version) were at one time taken to mean that a Christian should not buy anything by hire purchase, but should save up and make a purchase outright. Strange that in those days far more people than today lived in rented accommodation! The New International Version catches the sense of Paul's words with 'Let no debt remain outstanding'.

So much revision of opinion has taken place by Christians that we must be careful in our approach to Scripture, avoid making quick black-and-white judgements and recognize that we might conscientiously differ among ourselves on some points. In addition we know that those who are recognized as experts often differ among themselves. So when it comes to social, economic, political and green issues it becomes difficult for Christians to be sure of clear-cut positions (though this has not necessarily prevented some from arriving at them!). Yet all these are important matters, and all need to be considered in the light of biblical truth.

Three main approaches to coming to biblical answers can be mentioned. Firstly, we should ask what biblical *themes* bear on the particular matter? If we are thinking about ecology, themes such as these are important: 'The earth is the Lord's and all that is in it' (Psalm 24:1). Men and women are God's stewards of the resources he has given us (Genesis 1:28; 2:15). When Israel settled in Canaan the land with its resources was to be shared out equitably among the tribes (Numbers 34; Joshua 14–19). The earth is to be renovated so that Christians look forward to a new earth (2 Peter 3:13). And other themes could be mentioned. It is in the light of such as these that conclusions are to be reached.

Secondly, we should consider what *principles* we can find that will guide us in our thinking. God created Adam and Eve at the beginning. Several principles arise from this: the importance of the family as the basic unit of society; the unity of the human race; the equality of all men and women; marriage as monogamous and lifelong; children conceived and brought up within the orbit of the mutual love of husband and wife; and so on.

The distinction I am making is this. Themes are broader, they are more explicit and can usually be traced through Scripture. Principles are narrower, they underlie commands and practices, and as they do not lie on the surface, they often have to be deduced. At this point we might notice the use Paul makes of Deuteronomy 25:4, 'Do not muzzle an ox while it is treading out the grain.' In 1 Corinthians 9:8ff. he applies the principle behind this to preachers of the gospel, arguing that it is right for them to be supported financially by those to whom they minister. Just as it is right for the ox who does the labouring to share in the benefit of his work, so it is the same for those who work in the gospel.

Thirdly, we can look for *examples* which help us in determining what attitude to adopt. There are examples which show us the problems arising with polygamy (consider what we are told about Elkanah, Peninnah and Hannah in 1 Samuel 1:1–8). Exodus 21:22–25 is an example of the biblical attitude to the unborn child, and Proverbs 31:8–9 can be seen in the same light. The response of Paul and Silas in Acts 16:35–40 to the magistrates of Philippi is an example of holding those in authority to account.

Two further points are important. It is clear that the Bible sanctions proper research and learning from the world around us. When Jesus was replying to the Pharisees and Sadducees in Matthew 16:1–4 he was not criticizing them for being able to interpret the appearance of the skies, only for not understanding their times. We are expected to learn by observing the natural world and all that goes on in it, and to think through what we can see and deduce within a biblical framework. God has given us minds for this purpose. We need more Christians who can responsibly interact biblically with current knowledge, and who can distinguish between fact and theory, proper conclusions and baseless inferences.

Finally, I don't think it is always possible to come to definite decisions about the right and wrong of every issue that confronts us. There are areas where we have to come to what seems the best thing to do in the prevailing circumstances. Some Christians believe that the Bible forbids war, but most do not. Of those who believe in 'just war' as it is called, a number believe that the use of nuclear weapons can never be justified, in other words they believe in 'nuclear pacifism'. Christians have undoubtedly been divided over whether the 2003 war on Iraq was justified. My guess is that most British Christians doubt this, whereas most American Christians take the opposite view. This is not a theoretical matter. There are young Christian men and women in the armed forces. Are they right in following this career? Should they desert, or say they will not fight, if they disagree with a political decision to go to war? In other words I am saying that the Bible does not give absolute, definitive guidance on every issue. In some situations, we have to follow our own conscience responsibly before God, in submission to his Word as we understand it.

Applying the Bible to the nation

A great deal in the Old Testament was written for Israel as a nation. There were many commands and instructions that belonged to their corporate life. 'When you reap the harvest of your land, do not reap to the very edges of your field or gather the gleanings of your harvest … Leave them for the poor and alien.' 'When you enter the land and plant any kind of fruit tree … for three years … it must not be eaten. In the fourth year all its fruit will be holy … in the fifth year you may eat its fruit' (Leviticus 19:9–10, 23–25). We would not be likely to think that these commands were binding on us now, but we can see their wisdom, and can think of ways in which the principles they enshrine could be put into operation. We might also think that the first of these should inform our own legislation in its care for the poor, and look to see if our secular law reflects the same concern.

A further example occurs in Deuteronomy 22:8: 'When you build a new house, make a parapet around your roof so that you may not bring the guilt of bloodshed on your house if someone falls from the roof.' We can see underlying this command concern for a neighbour (see Leviticus 19:18), but also a responsibility to take proper precautions to protect life and limb. Failure to act responsibly makes a person guilty if an accident results.

When we come to consider applying biblical law, or biblical principle, to our own nation, we find it very difficult to be sure how, or even if, this is to be done. The past forty years or so have seen Christians fight to keep legislation that preserved Sunday as a Christian sabbath. This then became a campaign to keep Sunday special. Soon the question was how to ensure that Christians would not be compelled to work on Sundays. Now, many Christians do not think the sabbath command even applies to them, let alone to the nation. In a short period of time the evangelical consensus has radically changed, to the distress of those of us who believe in the continuing validity of the fourth commandment.

As this example shows, the question is a very relevant one, living as we do at a time when many laws based on Christian standards and principles are being systematically repealed. This is inevitable in days when Christianity has less and less influence on the mass of people and when attitudes are changing considerably. Precisely how we respond is beyond the scope of this book. What concerns us here is how this affects our understanding and application of the Bible. In considering this, these are the themes that need attention: what belongs to us as created beings; what is good for us and for society as a whole; what has been proved good and beneficial by experience, as well as having biblical precept; what protection minorities—like ourselves now—should have in a multi-cultural and supposedly tolerant society.

Christ in the Scriptures

We have already thought of some of the ways in which the Old Testament points to and speaks of Christ. The person and work of Jesus Christ lies at the heart of the biblical message, but we are only in a position to evaluate what the whole Bible says about him when we have the whole Bible before us. Undoubtedly the Old Testament speaks of him, and people like Abraham looked forward to his coming (see John 8:56). Nevertheless, because it is only in the light of the completed Scripture that we can fully understand the Old Testament, we look now at this subject. First some general considerations.

Enlarging our understanding of the Old Testament
Looking at the Old Testament in the light of the New and the coming of Christ does not diminish our understanding of the Old but rather expands it. What I mean is this. Everything that lies on the face of the Old Testament, and all the truths that we can see there and the lessons we can learn, are still valid and important. But viewing it all in the light of Jesus Christ adds a new dimension to it, opens up an enlarged understanding, giving us a whole new perspective.

It is important to look at it in this way. Sometimes the impression is given that reading the Old Testament as Christians means that we simply look for references to Christ. There are two dangers here. The first is that we may end up allegorizing Old Testament stories in order to make them refer to him. Unfortunately this has often been the case. I have come across some bizarre examples of this, and sadly the people concerned thought they had really gained some insight into the passages they used. 1 Kings 3:1 reads: 'Solomon made an alliance with Pharaoh king of Egypt and married his daughter.' This is not a foreshadowing of Christ 'marrying' a Gentile bride, the church! The second danger is that the intention of the author and the emphasis of the text are overlooked and important teaching can be set aside.

Take Genesis 1 as an example. In view of verses like John 1:3: 'Through him all things were made; without him nothing was made that has been made', and Hebrews 1:2: '… his [God's] Son … through whom he made the universe', it is proper to see the creative activity of the Son of God in Genesis 1. It is right to bear this in mind when you read that chapter, and to wonder at the truth that God's agent in creation is the one who took a human nature and died for us on the cross.

But the purpose of Genesis 1 is not to tell us about the Son in distinction from the Father. The chapter is about God the creator, and the creation which he called into being. It is also oriented against some of the false ideas of Moses' day; that there are many gods, for example; that the sun and moon are gods and to be worshipped; that different gods are in control of different powers of nature: the wind, the sea, the fertility of the land. Whatever belongs to the meaning of this passage needs to be understood and its significance taken to heart. And those who preach are to give full weight to these things. The doctrine of creation is absolutely fundamental and it is vital today. However—and here comes the enlargement—it is also important to remember that the Son of God was the agent in creation as well as our redeemer. The Son is Lord over creation; it bears witness to him, and our lives as created beings in a created world are to be lived with him and for him. It would be a grave mistake simply to identify creation with the Father and redemption with the Son.

Christ is God

For Christians the word 'God' refers to the triune God, Father, Son and Holy Spirit. When we read 'God' or 'Lord' in the Old Testament we should not think of these words in a non-trinitarian way as those not committed to Christianity do. Nor are we to identify God in the Old Testament as the Father, there is no warrant for restricting the word in that way. The word God, then, is not used in opposition to Christ, or more accurately in this context, the Son. As God, the Son is ever present in the Old Testament.

There is evidence to suggest that whenever God appeared to human beings in the Old Testament, he appeared in the person of the Son. Very often this is indicated by the term 'the angel of the LORD', a figure who is both identified with God and differentiated from him (see, for example, Genesis 16). It is certainly fitting that the divine person who was to become incarnate should be the one who appeared when God wished to converse with people prior to the incarnation. But we need to note that what took place on these occasions was an appearance of God, the triune God in the fullness of his being, in the Son. Jesus once said to Philip, 'Anyone who has seen me, has seen the Father' (John 14:9), and this is even more clearly the case in the Old Testament appearances of God. At Horeb it was 'the angel of the LORD' who appeared to Moses (Exodus 3:2). Yet this was not simply a revelation of the Son. It was a revelation of God, as the chapter makes clear. This is the God of Abraham, Isaac and Jacob and here the covenant name, 'I am who I am', is given.

All illustrations of the trinity are inadequate and some are positively misleading. In spite of that, I have found an illustration I heard many years ago of some help in thinking about this. If you think of a triangle that always has the same corner pointing towards you, you can apply that to the triune God. Just as it is the triangle you see, but always view it from the same corner, so we see God in his fullness but always viewed as he comes to us in the Son.

The word and Christ

Peter tells us that the prophets spoke by the Spirit of Christ when they spoke of the sufferings and glory of Christ (1 Peter 1:11). If the Holy Spirit is also the Spirit of Christ this means that the Old Testament is the Word of Christ to us. And when we read the Old Testament as Christians we read it as those who are in union with Jesus Christ and who live in fellowship with him.

Some of the teachers at my school had a great influence on their pupils. They were good teachers (if also strict) who knew their subjects and were enthusiastic about them and communicated well. Some of them had written the textbooks that we used. They knew precisely what the textbooks meant and they were able to explain the book, and the subject, in a direct and personal way. In an even more important way this is a picture of how Christians are to understand reading the Old Testament. We do so in fellowship with Christ, recognizing that he is teaching us from what he caused to be written for us.

The book of Proverbs, for example, has a great deal to say about ordinary life in a very down-to-earth way: '"It's no good, it's no good!" says the buyer; then off he goes and boasts about his purchase' (20:14). 'He who guards his mouth and his tongue keeps himself from calamity' (21:23). 'An anxious heart weighs a man down, but a kind word cheers him up' (12:25). Where is Christ in sayings like these? He isn't *there* in the sense that they point to him or tell us anything about his saving work. (Though many of them may tell us something about his own life and behaviour as a man— think of those occasions when Jesus said, 'Cheer up!' or, as the Authorized Version has it, 'Be of good cheer!') But he is there, or rather here with us, in the sense that it is he who has put interesting, provocative and practical sayings into this book and who helps us grasp their point and guides our lives as Christian people by them.

Christ and Jesus

In the first part of the book I have already briefly discussed the fact that in the Old Testament those who were anointed—'christs', if you like—all fell short of what they should have been. So while they pointed forward to the true and final Christ, Jesus himself, they also illustrated the need for a perfect Christ to come, one who would be all that God's anointed ought to be. We must take care, then, not to make a transference to Jesus of all that we are told about those who prefigured him. In all that the high priest did as high priest he prefigured what Jesus Christ was to do, though not in exactly the same way. Only Jesus offered *himself* as a sacrifice. But the high priest did not prefigure Jesus in his personal life. He was expected to marry, for example, and his son would be the next high priest. Neither David nor Solomon prefigured Jesus in their personal lives, nor did they always prefigure him in what they did in their official position as kings.

In my own mind I find it helpful to make a distinction between 'Christ' and 'Jesus' when I look at the Old Testament. 'Christ' is an official title, 'Jesus' is a personal name. There is a great deal about the Christ, the Messiah in the Old Testament. It all finds its fulfilment in Jesus, but the full person of Jesus himself is not there. David is not Jesus, Aaron is not Jesus, the temple is not Jesus, a slain lamb is not Jesus, but these persons and things point towards him, and find their fulfilment in him. So, as I pointed out earlier, there is no need to stumble at the idea of David as a picture of Jesus Christ. David as king exhibits the status and many of the functions of the Christ, but is not a full representation of Jesus. No one could be.

The story of redemption

As you get to know the Bible you begin to realize that though it comprises books of various sorts, written by different authors over some fifteen centuries, it has a strong story line. Three elements in this can be mentioned. First, the story is one of creation, disobedience, the calling of an individual and nation, failure, the coming of a Saviour and formation of a new people of God, and the promise of final and complete regeneration and glory yet to come. This first element can be enlarged upon, or reduced to a movement in four parts: creation, fall, redemption, consummation. Second, in this story God deals with people by covenant. Out of the wreckage left by human sin God pledges to give himself unreservedly in love to those whom he chooses—'I will be your God and you will be my people'. This is indicated by the very way in which we divide up the Bible, the Old Testament (or covenant) and the New Testament (or covenant). In this covenant it is God who calls, redeems and forms a people for himself. The Bible is the story of God in grace rescuing those who have sinned and bringing all creation to the destiny he prepared for it even from before its beginning.

The third element is that it is God himself who comes to rescue those who are lost and he does so in the person of the Son. This, of course, involved the incarnation and the life, ministry, sufferings, death and resurrection of Jesus Christ, who has been taken up to the throne of God and is even now working all things together to bring them to their predestined goal. So Jesus Christ has a central role in the Bible's story line. When we read the Old Testament it is not just a matter of looking at a book or passage as it is in itself. We should also ask, how does this fit in with the whole story, with the whole plan of God in salvation? And, because of the position he occupies in the story, in doing that we are actually asking how the passage relates to Jesus Christ.

For example, at first glance we might easily describe the book of Exodus as Israel coming out of Egypt and beginning the journey to the promised land. We might also see Moses as its central character. But on second thoughts we realize that actually it is the story of God delivering Israel from Egypt. It is the story of a great act of redeeming love by the God who had taken Israel into covenant with himself. Moses is a leader under God. He speaks God's Word, and leads at God's command. This is part of a story which leads up to the greatest act of God's redemption accomplished by Jesus Christ. We can see it, then, as an anticipation, a foreshadowing, of what is yet to come. The story pictures for us, and calls our attention to what God has done for us in rescuing us from a greater bondage than that of Egypt by a greater act of redemption accomplished by his Son, Jesus Christ.

Tracing Christ in the Old Testament

With these general points in mind we can go on to consider four ways in which we view Christ in the Old Testament.

First of all there are those occasions when God came to his people in a particular form. These are often called theophanies—appearances of God—though some prefer to speak of christophanies—appearances of Christ. It seems correct to view these as pre-incarnate appearances of the Son of God. Frequently, as already noted, the figure who appears is called the angel of the LORD. Isaiah 63:9 speaks of 'the angel of his presence', signifying the presence of God with the Israelites when they came out of Egypt and travelled through the desert. 1 Corinthians 10:4 refers to Christ as the 'spiritual rock that accompanied them'. It is perhaps especially significant that it was the angel of the LORD who came to Elijah while he was under the broom tree (1 Kings 19:3–9), and ministered so compassionately to him.

Second—and we now see how the Old Testament looks forward to Christ as the one to come—there are specific promises and prophecies about his coming. The New Testament indicates many of these. We do not have to go very far in Matthew before we come across, 'All this took place to fulfil what the Lord had said through the prophet' (1:22). In some cases we need to look carefully at what the New Testament writers say in order to understand how they come to refer particular verses to Christ. This is the case in Matthew 2:15,17–18,23. Thoughtful study will show us why Matthew wrote as he did, and helps us in understanding how the New Testament writers used the Old Testament.

We need not think that we are to refer to Christ only those Old Testament passages which the New Testament does. We can, rather, follow the New Testament pattern. For example, as John 13:18 applies Psalm 41:9 ('He who shares my bread has lifted up his heel against me') to Judas Iscariot's betrayal of Jesus, it seems legitimate to understand Psalm 55:12–14 in the same way. And very often the fact that a verse is used as a prophecy indicates that a whole passage can be understood in that way. Isaiah 53 is an example of this. However, this is by no means always the case. John 2:17 applies Psalm 69:9 ('zeal for your house consumes me') to Jesus, but it will hardly do to apply verse 5 in the same psalm to him ('You know my folly, O God; my guilt is not hidden from you'). We have to use judgement in these cases. David can be speaking of himself, yet in places the Holy Spirit enabled him to speak words which are more fully and completely true of Christ.

Third—and here we pick up something we have already considered—because Christ means 'anointed one' prophets, priests and kings—who were all anointed—point forward to the Christ. What they did partially and often inadequately, Jesus did fully and perfectly.

Finally, the whole sacrificial system, including priest, altar, sacrifice, tabernacle and temple all point forward to Jesus Christ and the perfect atonement he was to make by the one offering of himself. So we read Exodus, Leviticus and Numbers in the light of the letter to the Hebrews.

These are little more than pointers to the way in which we are to read the Old Testament as Christians and to see how it prepares for and points towards Jesus Christ.

While Christ is at the centre of the whole Bible, he is also the gift of the Father's love and it is the Holy Spirit's particular work to glorify him (John 16:14). The grand story of the Bible, and the great redemption of which it tells, reveals a tri-personal God, Father, Son and Holy Spirit, who in oneness and threeness loves, saves, glorifies and will be all in all for ever.

Review and further study

1. Think about the differences between studying, reading and meditating upon a biblical passage. How much time do you give to meditating upon the Bible?
2. How can someone gain awareness of his or her own presuppositions? Are there any steps you can take to free yourself from them?

3. How can you positively prepare yourself to let the Bible speak to you on its own terms? Do you always consider the response a passage is calling for?
4. Consider what it means to be a member of the church. What bearing does this have on understanding the Bible and on the Christian life?
5. What difference does the coming of Christ make to applying the Old Testament? What guidance does the New Testament give for applying the Old Testament today?
6. In what ways do we discover Christ in the Old Testament?

To think about or discuss

Consider Genesis 30:1. Would it be legitimate to apply Rachel's demand of Jacob to a Christian minister or church pleading with Christ for converts in the face of the apparent success of a cultic group or heretical church?

Do applications of national laws in the Old Testament that arise from considering the principles they exemplify (see the example given on p. 113 from Deuteronomy 22:8) have the same authority as moral laws?

Postscript

This book is now finished, but it is really an introduction. Hopefully those who have read it will have found it helpful, but will also desire to study the subject further. A select bibliography follows this paragraph. In writing I have been conscious of wanting to achieve several goals. Firstly, I have wanted to enlarge understanding of the task of interpretation. That is one reason for speaking about the three 'worlds'. There is more to interpretation than the application of a few principles. Secondly, I have also wanted to underline the literary character of the Bible. Unless one understands something about the different genres and the way these work, one's understanding of much of the Bible is likely to be restricted. Thirdly, I have wanted to stress the role of the reader. How we approach the Bible makes a great difference to our understanding and appreciation of it. We need a spiritual, sensitive approach that depends on the Spirit and is ready to respond to what the Bible says. Finally, I want to encourage enjoyment in reading the Bible as well as understanding. Reading the Bible is not a chore. The Bible is interesting, true to life, instructive, delightful. Of course, there are very solemn and serious parts—exposure of sin and warning of judgement are an essential part of its message. But overall it is a message of mercy; it leads us to rejoice in God and to praise his name.

Select bibliography

Gordon D. Fee and Douglas Stuart, *How to Read the Bible for all its Worth* (London: Scripture Union, 1994) [provocative]

Richard L. Pratt, *He Gave Us Stories* (Presbyterian and Reformed, 1993) [informative]

Leland Ryken, *Words of Life* (Grand Rapids: Baker, 1987) [NT, delightful]

Leland Ryken, *Words of Delight* (Grand Rapids: Baker, 2nd ed. 1993) [OT, delightful]

D.A. Carson, *Exegetical Fallacies* (Grand Rapids: Baker, 2nd ed. 1996) [cautionary]

Warren W. Wiersbe, *Preaching and Teaching with Imagination* (Grand Rapids: Baker, 1994) [fascinating]

William W. Klein, Craig L. Blomberg, Robert L. Hubbard, *Introduction to Biblical Interpretation* (Nelson, 1993) [comprehensive]

Gerald Bray, *Biblical Interpretation Past and Present* (Leicester: IVP, Apollos, 1996) [historical heavyweight]